From Courts to Dungeons:

Classical Monologues for Men and Women

ALSO BY MARTIN JAGO

ESL Shakespeare Everyday Phrases
To Play of Not to Play, 50 Games for Acting Shakespeare

From Courts to Dungeons:

Classical Monologues for Men and Women

Edited with notes and analysis by

MARTIN JAGO

A Smith and Kraus Book   2018

A Smith and Kraus Book
177 Lyme Road, Hanover, NH 03755
Editorial 603.643.6431 To Order 1.877.668.8680
www.smithandkraus.com

From Courts to Dungeons:
Classical Monologues for Men and Women
Copyright © 2017 by Martin Jago
All rights reserved.

Manufactured in the United States of America

ISBN: 9781575259178
Library of Congress Control Number: 2017958266

Typesetting and layout by Elizabeth E. Monteleone
Cover by Olivia Monteleone

For information about custom editions, special sales, education and corporate purchases, please contact Smith and Kraus at editor@smithandkraus.com or 603.643.6431

To Alexander McConnell
A dear friend and fine actor

CONTENTS

The Monologues

ELIZABETHAN AGE (1558 – 1603)

JACOBEAN AGE (1603 – 1625)

CAROLINE AGE (1625 – 1649)

ACKNOWLEDGEMENTS

Thank you to my agents Janet Rosen and Sheree Bykofsky for their support, advice, and guidance. My gratitude also to Marisa Smith and the whole Smith and Kraus team for their hard work and dedication.

My sincerest gratitude to Lisa Wolpe, an extraordinary actress, theatre artist, and the Producing Artistic Director of Los Angeles Women's Shakespeare Company. In her excellent foreword to this book she expertly deconstructs and examines the actor's audition, offering insight, humor, and most importantly, sage advice.

To those artists, educators, and fellow theatre makers who kindly provided endorsements for this book—Jennifer Sandella, Suzanne Hunt, Sabra Williams, Bernie C. Byrnes, Dathan B. Williams, Rob Nagle, and Stuart W. Howard—many thanks. Among them, Dathan B. Williams also provided invaluable feedback, support, and critical responses that helped shape the introduction to this book. I am most grateful.

I am thankful to Virtic Emil Brown and Russell Blakey for their generosity in giving permission for the use of their images on the cover of the book.

Thanks also to the many fine actors at Classical Theatre Lab in Los Angeles for their input and advice during the research stage of this book.

A special thank you to actor Roger Clark for his help, advice, and recommendations.

While researching material for this book I spent time in the Literature Department of Los Angeles Public Library's Central Library where the help and support of staff, not least Jim Sherman, was exceptional. Thank you.

From my heart, thank you to Demelza and Jeffrey.

I owe a debt of gratitude to Clare Morgan, Jane Draycott, Amal Chatterjee, and the excellent tutors on the Master's Program in Creative Writing at University of Oxford.

Thanks also to Alexander McConnell, Kevin Logan, Andy and Nicky Hallett, Darren Feltham, Paul Ireland, Julian Lewis-

Jones, Bernard Collins, Andrew and Kim Allen-King, Steve and Ros Davis, Derek Jones, Michael "2032" Skaf, and Paddy Campanaro. Fine friends, one and all.

Thanks to Marilyn Le Conte for her support. Hello too, Dave Bond and all the Royal Welsh College of Music and Drama actors—then, now, and tomorrow—for their creative spark, professionalism, and dedication to the craft of acting.

To my family: Mum, Dad, Tim, Nicola, Sunee, Kaite, Dean, aunts, uncles, cousins, and to my grandmother Phyllis Rogers M.P. (*Master of Pastry*), love and gratitude.

FOREWORD

You never get a second chance to make a first impression. In the two minutes of extreme intensity that occur when you audition for a part in a play, you must excel at bringing the character to life in an impressive and moving way. You've got to present with passion and skill, balance the personal and political, and portray arguments with emotional truth. All this must be achieved while balancing rhetorical skill with vulnerability, and aligning your words with the blood pounding through you to the beat of your heart.

You need to find a piece of text that requires you to delve, with great stakes, into the survival and betterment of your own humanity and the world at large.

Martin Jago takes the subject of classical monologues into new territory, offering the reader a fine selection of pieces that explore the prisoner's plight…in eminently playable ways. Mr. Jago has assembled a fascinating array of desperate, divine, and achingly human characters whose spirited words are filled with life and death-defying courage.

Each monologue in this collection offers the combatant a fine horse and the sword Excalibur with which to plunge into the inexorable forces of "the oppressor's wrong…the law's delay" and "the insolence of office" as Hamlet does in his most famous soliloquy. And yet, as brilliant as Hamlet's "to be or not to be" speech is, the fear that the director may have heard these words too often may alarm you.

WHAT TO DO?

Within these pages a range of possibilities exist. These texts are gifts to actors who yearn to connect with the complexity of life. Don't worry about how famous a piece is or count how many other actors have flung themselves at the same mark and fallen short of a perfect performance. Trust that there will be something of your mind, soul, and heart revealed in your valiant attempt. Still, it might be refreshing for you to discover within these pages pieces unknown where footprints mark no well-worn path to the "undiscovered country."

Themes of confinement, injustice, and power are found throughout this book; more than fifty pieces on the subject are grouped in an invaluable collection of brilliant and in many cases, seldom-heard pieces.

And may I add, regarding the division of male and female monologues listed herein, a challenge to explore them all. What better way to defy expectation as an actress stepping into the fray than to redefine *Hamlet* through your unique interpretation of the role? Or have you, as an actor, ever considered imaginatively *unsexing* yourself in an attempt at Lady Macbeth?

In today's more widely accepted gender spectrum, now celebrated on international stages, the call to liberate one's self from traditional gender boxes and their forced expectations is raging like wildfire. Certainly, to Shakespeare's all-male troupe this gender-bending practice was the norm.

All-female, all-male, trans and gender-reversed productions of the classics are bringing power, brilliance, and new perspectives on stage every day, exciting audiences worldwide in a wonderful exploration of identity in performance.

In my experience (having, I believe, played more of the male roles than any actress in history), one can change the game and break all the rules by simply following your passion for the role and playing it with a no-holds-Bard commitment that will redefine the field. In fact, dare I say, the field has been won. Follow your hearts – I wish you the joy of the word!

Lisa Wolpe,
Producing Artistic Director,
Los Angeles Women's Shakespeare Company.

INTRODUCTION

This unique collection of classical monologues for men and women celebrates the literary strength of the Elizabethan and Jacobean stage, including writers who seldom escape the shadow of Shakespeare's glory, yet who have provided some of the finest dramatic writing in the English language. *From Courts to Dungeons* is unique in other ways too. Unlike many monologue books, it unifies the speeches in a body of work that is linked by setting. As the title suggests, the drama in this book comes from the distinct perspective of characters caught in the most desperate of circumstances: victims or victors, they are all in the grip of the justice system, be it on trial or languishing in prison, facing execution or standing guard.

From Courts to Dungeons reflects the obsession of an age. Imprisonment, torture, and execution were present and real dangers to Londoners of the 1500s and 1600s. There were around eighteen prisons in London at the time, many of which were known to writers like Jonson, Dekker, and Kyd. There was a prison for debtors, one for prostitutes, another for felons, a prison for religious offenders, one for those awaiting execution, many others, and of course The Tower of London, a prison reserved for those from the higher echelons of society, but a prison none the less. Prisoners paid for their keep or languished. Bribery was commonplace and prisons made money on the backs of the incarcerated.

There are obvious parallels with our own times in which prisons are run as profit-making businesses and the most powerful country on earth incarcerates more of its citizens than any other country in the world. Meanwhile, state-sanctioned torture is condoned and on the rise around the globe, making *From Courts to Dungeons* a timely collection of classical monologues with contemporary resonances.

Some of the speeches in this collection include composite speeches in which interjectory lines of other characters have been cut. Always refer to the original text where possible to gain a fuller knowledge of the material in its original context.

REGARDING GENDER

Sometimes, actors walk into rehearsal rooms and perform a little alchemy – transforming a brief passage of time (usually no more than three minutes) into an audition that is both striking and memorable. Every director waits in anticipation of such moments, never quite sure what to expect, no matter how well the headshot matches the face or the resume reflects the actor's achievements. The real proof always lies in the quality and craft of the performance.

One essential element of that alchemical magic is the audition material. Performed well, the piece should be self-explanatory, despite being culled from the wider context of a full-length play. Even those directors with an encyclopedic knowledge of plays and audition pieces will encounter material that is new to them. Therefore, a two or three-minute audition piece should provide enough of a journey to give its audience clues as to where the character has come from and where they are heading, both literally and figuratively.

Furthermore, the character and actor should be well-suited. That doesn't mean one always needs to adhere to casting orthodoxy in terms of age and look but it does mean, I feel, that the actor should have an affinity for the material and that it should capture aspects of the actor's range and ability.

Regarding gender, classical drama provides greater flexibility than contemporary material since it lies outside the convention of Naturalism that dictates male actors play male roles and vice versa. This is a particularly important consideration for female actors because while some female characters do occasionally shine (in speeches that are few and far between) in classical texts, countless female actors have already done those speeches to death.

We know that men played both male and female roles on the Elizabethan stage, and characters from the world of Elizabethan and Jacobean drama speak in poetry more than prose, frequently breaking the fourth wall with asides to the audience, so would a female Hamlet really be a stretch of the imagination? Sarah Bernhardt played the role both on stage and film as early as 1899. Further back still, actress Charlotte Charke played the part and many other male roles in the 18th century.

In recent times, cross-gender casting has given us some celebrated performances, from Glenda Jackson's recent *King Lear* at the Old Vic in London, Maxine Peake's *Hamlet* at the Royal Exchange, Harriet Walter's *Henry IV* at the Donmar Warehouse, while in Los Angeles, actress Lisa Wolpe has won numerous accolades, managing to rack up more performances of male Shakespeare roles than any other actress on the planet.

For the men of course, it's business as usual while such cross-gender choices remain far more difficult for the contemporary female actor than they ought to be. Happily, this collection of dramatic monologues also contains numerous female character speeches, many of which are relatively unknown yet wrought from the finest writing of the age.

RACE

Besides Othello, Aaron from Shakespeare's *Titus Andronicus* is one of very few characters of color represented in Elizabethan and Jacobean drama. For some, this scarcity of representation forms the basis of a convenient excuse for a lack of racial diversity in the casting of classical plays.

Aaron's villainy is so egregious, his actions so barbarous and full of hate that in many ways the character can be viewed as simply holding a mirror, as 'twere, up to the nature of accepted racial stereotypes. And thus, if actors of color are only ever cast to play violent roles, we will forever continue to perpetuate stereotypical viewpoints of people of color.

It wasn't until 2016 that that most venerated of Shakespeare companies, The Royal Shakespeare Company, first cast a black actor in the role of Hamlet. Why did we have to wait so long? Arguments claiming that exclusion is simply based on deference to some original way of doing things are spurious. By that same reckoning, actors of color would never perform in a Shakespeare play and neither would women. By the same principles, every production would have to take place outside, before sunset, and with the merest suggestion of a set.

How fitting that the brilliance of Paapa Essiedu's performance in the title role of the RSC production had the power to shatter prejudices, leaving the world in no doubt that Shakespeare and his contemporaries belong to one and all of us.

If theatre is to reflect the diversity of our culture rather than its prejudices, we need to be loud and clear about it, beginning with this most prevalent of casting biases.

As for Aaron the Moor, the speech of his that I have included in this collection focuses on the one moment in the play when Shakespeare chooses to present the character as a caring father, full of love and compassion for his son.

AUDITION PREPARATION

- Choose a piece that speaks to you, that sparks your imagination, provokes your acting senses, challenges you, and which somehow feels like the right fit.
- Do your homework, read the play, know the story, understand how your character arrives at this point, and what happens to them in the chain of events that follow.
- Learn the piece inside out.
- Make clear acting choices. Think in verbs. What does your character want and from whom?
- How high are the stakes? The scene isn't just about what your character wants but how badly they want it.
- Is your character addressing another character, themselves, god, the audience, or a combination of all four?
- Think about the journey of the piece. Consider where it starts and how the shifts that occur within the monologue propel it towards its conclusion. The dynamic shape of the piece is central to its success. If it's all on one level physically or emotionally, add variety but have clear reasons for making changes. Whatever emotions a character experiences: love, betrayal, rage, or any number of other human feelings, there are endless shades and expressions to each.
- Remain flexible. A director might enjoy a well-crafted audition piece but that doesn't tell them how well you take direction. Listen carefully and be prepared to take on board whatever changes a director asks you to make to the piece.
- Work the piece.

• Get feedback on your work in progress. Seek out constructive criticism. Despite acting being the most collaborative of art forms, when it comes to audition material why do we expect actors to fend for themselves?

AUDITION ETIQUETTE

The following points may be obvious but it's worth taking a moment to consider them again. Too often, actors wrong foot themselves with the most rudimentary audition steps.

• Be friendly, calm, confident and professional.
• Dress for an audition not for dinner with the Queen of England. Maintain a professional appearance but wear loose-fitting, comfortable clothes for the rehearsal room.
• If there aren't twelve people staring back at you from behind a desk or a six foot drop and several rows of stalls between you and the director, shake hands.
• Remember, your audition has to fit the space. You may have rehearsed the piece in a small room or rehearsal studio only to step into a two-thousand seat auditorium for your audition. Be prepared to make the necessary adjustments (vocally and physically).
• Introduce the piece briefly i.e. name of character, act, scene, and play (and author unless completely obvious – no one needs to be told that *Hamlet* was written by Shakespeare).
• Take a moment to centre yourself.
• Maintain focus (despite the wailing of fire trucks outside or construction work next door).
• Take a beat at the end of the piece, hold the moment before stepping out of character.
• Listen and respond politely to any questions.
• Follow any direction given.

A BRIEF WORKING GUIDE TO BLANK VERSE

Many of the speeches in this collection are written in blank verse – unrhymed iambic pentameter. Writing in verse was the convention of the day and blank verse conforms to a simple rule of rhythm that resembles the pattern of ordinary speech in the

English language. By discarding rhyme but maintaining the poetic beat, the effect of blank verse on the listener is that the language often feels natural yet poetic, heightened yet not overstated.

Iambic pentameter is a line of poetry in which every other syllable is stressed. There are ten syllables per line. For example, the following two lines are written in blank verse:

I drove by Jason's house the other day.
He's painted all the walls and roof bright pink.

I feel for Jason's neighbors, I really do. Let's examine the lines a little closer. I have highlighted the stressed beats this time:

I **drove** by **Ja**son's **house** the **oth**er **day**.
He's **paint**ed **all** the **walls** and **roof** bright **pink**!

When working on a blank-verse speech don't worry about the meter. Simply start by reading the piece out loud a couple of times. More than likely you will instinctively navigate a path through the speech, highlighting all the important parts of the text as you go. But having done this a couple of times and gained a 'feel' for the piece, it is worth following a simple exercise: write the speech out with a space between each line and mark each unstressed and stressed syllable. As an example, I have used Portia's 'quality of mercy' speech from *The Merchant of Venice*. (No book that references Shakespeare and the justice system could do without it).

Act IV, sc. i:
Portia, disguised as a lawyer's apprentice, Balthazar, addresses Shylock and the court, answering Shylock's question as to why he should show mercy to Antonio. She explains that mercy is not handed over grudgingly but bestowed freely because it's the right thing to do.

It is a wonderful speech and for that reason, very well-known, which raises a potential dilemma for the actor. *To do or not to do? That is the question.* Some would advise steering well clear of the 'famous' speeches in favor of lesser known marvels. Others might argue that since the piece is so often avoided it is time to breathe new life into it. I would add that if the glove fits, wear it!

PORTIA:
The **qual**-i-**ty** of **mer**cy **is** not **strained**.
○ ● ○ ● ○ ● ○ ● ○ ●

It **drop**peth **as** the **gen**tle **rain** from **heav**en
○ ● ○ ● ○ ● ○ ● ○ ● ○

Up**on** the **place** be**neath**. It **is** twice **blest**:
○ ● ○ ● ○ ● ○ ● ○ ●

It **bless**eth **him** that **gives** and **him** that **takes**.
○ ● ○ ● ○ ● ○ ● ○ ●

'Tis **might**iest **in** the **might**iest. **It** be**comes**
○ ● ○ ● ○ ● ○ ● ○ ●

The **throne**d **mon**arch **bet**ter **than** his **crown**.
○ ● ○ ● ○ ● ○ ● ○ ●

His **scep**tre **shows** the **force** of **temp**oral **pow**er,
○ ● ○ ● ○ ● ○ ● ○ ● ○

The **at**-tri-**bute** to **awe** and **maj**-es-**ty,**
○ ● ○ ● ○ ● ○ ● ○ ●

Where**in** doth **sit** the **dread** and **fear** of **kings**,
○ ● ○ ● ○ ● ○ ● ○ ●

But **mer**cy **is** ab**ove** this **scep**tered **sway**.
○ ● ○ ● ○ ● ○ ● ○ ●

It **is** en**throne**d **in** the **hearts** of **kings**;
○ ● ○ ● ○ ● ○ ● ○ ●

It **is** an **at**-tri-**bute** to **God** him**self**,
○ ● ○ ● ○ ● ○ ● ○ ●

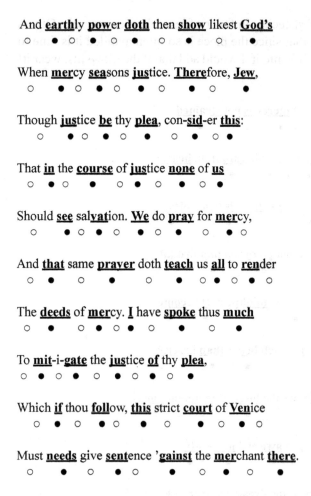

And **earth**ly **pow**er **doth** then **show** likest **God's**

When **mer**cy **sea**sons **jus**tice. **There**fore, **Jew**,

Though **jus**tice **be** thy **plea**, con-**sid**-er **this**:

That **in** the **course** of **jus**tice **none** of **us**

Should **see** sal**va**tion. **We** do **pray** for **mer**cy,

And **that** same **prayer** doth **teach** us **all** to **ren**der

The **deeds** of **mer**cy. **I** have **spoke** thus **much**

To **mit**-i-**gate** the **jus**tice **of** thy **plea**,

Which **if** thou **foll**ow, **this** strict **court** of **Ven**ice

Must **needs** give **sent**ence '**gainst** the **mer**chant **there**.

You might have noticed that the speech doesn't strictly conform to the rule of ten unstressed/stressed syllables throughout. Poets added variety to the lines with a number of variations. An iambic foot of unstressed/stressed syllables is sometimes replaced with a stressed/unstressed (trochaic foot) sequence. Other lines have an extra unstressed syllable added to the end (such as lines 2, 7, 17, 18 and 21). Punctuation adds yet more variety to the line.

Words with 'ed' endings deserve attention. To fit the meter of a line they are sometimes voiced. Portia's speech gives us some examples of this 'ed' voicing. In line six the word 'throned' is pronounced 'throne-ed.'

The **thron**ed **mon**arch **bet**ter **than** his **crown**.
○ ● ○ ● ○ ● ○ ● ○ ●

Without voicing the 'ed' ending of the word, the line would contain only nine syllables and disrupt the flow of iambs. The same happens in line eleven with the word 'enthroned':

It **is** en**thron**ed **in** the **hearts** of **kings**;
○ ● ○ ● ○ ● ○ ● ○ ●

At the same time, it is necessary to avoid voicing some other 'ed' word endings in the speech. In the following example from line ten the word 'sceptered' appears. It must be voiced as two syllables not three since a voiced 'ed' ending would add an additional stressed syllable to the line, breaking the rule of five stresses that pentameter demands.

But **mer**cy **is** ab**ove** this **scep**tered **sway**.
○ ● ○ ● ○ ● ○ ● ○ ●

The process of taking a pen or pencil and doing this blank verse detective work is called 'scansion.' It is important because the playwright wants us to pay particular attention to some words (and ideas) more than others.

No one is suggesting that every script or speech is marked up in this way or that having done so, every speech is performed mechanically by coming down hard on every stressed beat. However, as an exercise, it is worth trying this out loud and comparing it with a reading that attempts to discard the meter. By finding the middle ground between these two versions, the meter seems to mark itself and one becomes aware of its presence treading heavily through some lines while tiptoeing through others.

Here endeth the lesson.

The Monologues

In Memory

ELIZABETHAN AGE (1558 – 1603)

THOMAS OF WOODSTOCK or RICHARD II, PART ONE
by Anon

Character:	Tresilian, male, a flatterer and inveigler in the court of Richard II.
Playing age:	20s – 30s.
Act 1, Sce 2:	Tresilian has been named Lord Chief Justice of England. In the company of his friends he talks of exploiting his position to favor them. When they leave, he gives a soliloquy revealing his plans to be a truly evil Lord Chief Justice.

TRESILIAN:
Hum, hum, hum, legit° or non legit?
Methinks already I sit upon the bench
With dreadful frowns frighting° the lousy rascals,
And when the jury once cries "guilty"
Could pronounce "Lord have mercy on thee"
With a brow as rough and stern as surly
Rhadamanth;° or when a fellow talks
Cry "Take him, jailor; clap bolts of iron
On his heels and hands." Chief Justice, my lords.
Hum, hum, hum.
I will wear the office in his true ornament.
How sir, to punish you, the minions to the king,
The jewels of his heart, his dearest loves?
'Zounds, I will screw and wind the stubborn law
To any fashion that shall like you best.
It shall be law, what I shall say is law,
And what's most suitable to all your pleasures.

[Exit the others. TRESILIAN remains.]

So let them pass° Tresilian, now bethink thee,
Hum, Lord Chief Justice; methinks already
I am swelled more plump than erst° I was.
Authority's a dish that feeds men fat,
An excellent delicate: Yet best be wise,

No state's secure without some enemies.
The dukes will frown; why I can look as grim
As John of Gaunt, and all that frown with him.
But yet until mine office be put on°
By kingly Richard, I'll conceal myself,
Framing such subtle laws that Janus-like°
May with a double face salute them both;
I'll search my brain and turn the leaves of law.
Wit makes us great, greatness keeps fools in awe.

legit: legitimate. *frighting:* frightening. **Rhadamanth:** from Greek
mythology; one of the judges of the dead. **pass:** leave. *erst:* previously.
put on: make demands of. **Janus-like:** from Greek mythology; Janus
had two faces.

THOMAS OF WOODSTOCK or RICHARD II, PART ONE
by Anon

Character:	Thomas of Woodstock, Duke of Gloucester, male. King Richard's uncle. Forthright, honorable, and not shy of telling the young king where he is going wrong. He has no time for the court flatterers whom Richard favors.
Playing age:	Late 40s – 60s.
Act 5, Sce 1:	Arrested and taken to Calais, Woodstock knows he will soon die. It is falsely suggested to him by Lapoole, who is there to oversee Woodstock's imminent murder, that if he simply asks for forgiveness from the king, it will be granted. Woodstock asks for a pen and paper to write to the king.

WOODSTOCK:
For what should I submit or ask his mercy?
Had I offended, with all low submission
I'd lay my neck under the block before him
And willingly endure the stroke of death.
But if not so, why should my fond entreaties°
Make my true loyalty appear like treason?
No, no, Lapoole, let guilt men beg pardons.
My mind is clear. And I must tell ye, sir,
Princes have hearts like pointed diamonds
That will in sunder° burst afore they bend,
And such lives here, though death King Richard sends.
Yet fetch me pen and ink; I'll write to him
Not to entreat, but to admonish him
That he forsake his foolish ways in time
And learn to govern like a virtuous prince:
Call home his wise and reverent counselors,
Thrust from his court those cursed flatterers
That hourly work the realm's confusion.
This counsel, if he follow, may in time
Pull down those mischiefs that so fast do climb.

entreaties: petitions. *in sunder:* in pieces.

THE SPANISH TRAGEDY
by Thomas Kyd

Character:	Hieronimo, male. Knight Marshal of Spain, loyal to the king yet bent on bloody revenge for the death of his son.
Playing age:	40s – 50s.
Act 3, Sce 6:	In his role as a Justice, Hieronimo must oversee an execution. He reflects on the irony of carrying out justice for others while unable to find it for his son.

HIERONIMO:

Thus must we toil in other men's extremes,°
That know not how to remedy our own,
And do them justice, when unjustly we,
For all our wrongs° can compass° no redress.
But shall I never live to see the day,
That I may come by justice of the heavens
To know the cause that may my cares allay?
This toils my body, this consumeth age,°
That only I to all men just must be,
And neither gods nor men be just to me.
But come for that we came for: let's begin;
For here lies that which bids me to be gone.
Stand forth, thou monster, murderer of men;
And here, for satisfaction of the world,
Confess thy folly and repent thy fault;
For there's thy place of execution.
For blood with blood shall, while I sit as judge,
Be satisfied, and the law discharged.
And though myself cannot receive the like,
Yet will I see that others have their right.
Dispatch: the fault's° approved and confessed,
And by our law he is condemned to die.

---

extremes: hardships. *wrongs*: injustices suffered. *compass*: get. *consumeth age*: shorten life. *fault*: crime.

Martin Jago

TAMBURLAINE THE GREAT, PART ONE
by Christopher Marlowe

Character:	Zabina, female. Wife of Bajazeth, Emperor of the Turks. A proud and arrogant queen who has been captured and enslaved.
Playing age:	20s – 40s.
Act 5, Sce 2:	With her husband Bajazeth caged, Zabina has been enslaved by Tamburlaine, and both her and her husband have been taunted, mocked, and abused by him. Alone with Bajazeth, she laments their unbearable circumstances.

ZABINA:

Then is there left no Mahomet, no God,
No fiend, no fortune, nor no hope of end
To our infamous, monstrous slaveries?
Gape, earth, and let the fiends infernal view
A hell as hopeless and as full of fear
As are the blasted banks of Erebus,°
Where shaking ghosts with ever-howling groans
Hover about the ugly ferryman
To get a passage to Elysium.
Why should we live O wretches, beggars, slaves,
Why live we, Bajazeth, and build° up nests
So high within the region of the air
By living long in this oppression,
That all the world will see and laugh to scorn
The former triumphs of our mightiness
In this obscure infernal servitude?

Erebus: hell. **build...air**: build up false hopes.

TAMBURLAINE THE GREAT, PART ONE
by Christopher Marlowe

Character: Zabina, female. Wife of Bajazeth, Emperor of the Turks. A proud and arrogant queen who has been captured and enslaved.

Playing age: 20s – 40s.

Act 5, Sce 2:   She returns from fetching water to find Bajazeth has killed himself by smashing his head against his cage.

ZABINA:

What do mine eyes behold, my husband dead?
His skull all riven in twain, his brains dashed out?
The brains of Bajazeth, my lord and sovereign!
O Bajazeth, my husband and my lord,

O Bajazeth, O Turk, O emperor, give him his liquor? Not I.
Bring milk and fire, and my blood I bring him again. Tear
me in pieces, give me the sword with a ball of wild-fire upon
it! Down with him, down with him! Go to my child, away,
away, away! Ah, save that infant, save him, save him! I,
even I, speak to her – the sun was down. Streamers white, red,
black, here, here, here! Fling the meat in his face! Taburlaine,
Tamburlaine, let the soldiers be buried. Hell, death, Tamburlaine, hell, make ready my coach, my chair, my jewels, I come,
I come, I come!

[She runs against the cage and brains herself.]

TAMBURLAINE THE GREAT, PART ONE
by Christopher Marlowe

Character:	Bajazeth, male. Emperor of the Turks. Proud, unyielding, he is deeply despairing of his fate at the hands of Tamburlaine.
Playing age:	30s – 50s.
Act 5, Sce 2:	Caged by Tamburlaine, used as his footstool, mocked, taunted, and abused, alone with his wife Zabina, Bajazeth angrily laments their fall from greatness.

BAJAZETH:

O life more loathsome to my vexed thoughts
Than noisome parbreak° of the Stygian snakes,
Which fills the nooks of hell with standing° air,
Infecting all the ghosts with cureless griefs!
O dreary engines° of my loathed sight,
That see my crown, my honour and my name
Thrust under yoke and thraldom of a thief,
Why feed ye still on day's accursed beams
And sink not quite into my tortured soul?
You see my wife, my queen, and emperess,
Brought up and propped by the hand of fame,
Queen of fifteen contributory queens,
Now thrown to rooms of black abjection,°
Smeared with blots of basest drudgery,
And villainess° to shame, disdain and misery.
Accursed Bajazeth, whose words of ruth°
That would with pity cheer Zabina's heart
And make our souls resolve° in ceaseless tears,
Sharp hunger bites upon and gripes the root
From whence the issues of my thoughts do break.
O poor Zabina, O my queen, my queen!
Fetch me some water for my burning breast,
To cool and comfort me with longer date,
That, in the shortened sequel of my life
I may pour forth my soul into thine arms

With words of love, whose moaning intercourse
Hath hitherto been stayed with wrath and hate
Of our expressless° banned inflictions.

parbreak: vomit. ***standing***: stagnant. ***engines***: eyes. ***abjection***: shame.
villainess: servant. ***ruth***: despair. ***resolve***: dissolve. ***expressless***: inde-
scribable.

Martin Jago

TAMBURLAINE THE GREAT, PART ONE
by Christopher Marlowe

Character:	Bajazeth, male. Emperor of the Turks. Proud, unyielding, yet deeply despairing of his fate at the hands of Tamburlaine.
Playing age:	30s – 50s.
Act 5, Sce 2:	Caged, taunted, and abused by Tamburlaine, Bajazeth finally resolves to kill himself by smashing his brains against his cage.

BAJAZETH:
Now Bajazeth, abridge thy baneful days,
And beat the brains out of thy conquered head,
Since other means are all forbidden me
That may be ministers of my decay.
O highest lamp of ever-living Jove,
Accursed day infected with my griefs,
Hide now thy stained face in endless night
And shut the windows of the lightsome heavens.
Let ugly Darkness with her rusty coach
Engirt° with tempests, wrapped in pitchy clouds
Smother the earth with never-fading mists,
And let her horses from their nostrils breathe
Rebellious winds and dreadful thunderclaps,
That in this terror Tamburlaine may live,
And my pined° soul, resolved in liquid air,
May still excruciate his tormented thoughts.
Then let the stony dart of senseless cold
Pierce through the centre of my withered heart
And make a passage for my loathed life.

[He brains himself against the cage.]

engirt: encircle, envelop. **pined**: tormented.

TAMBURLAINE THE GREAT, PART TWO
by Christopher Marlowe

Character:	Callapine, male. Son of Bajazeth and heir to the Turkish Empire. Bold, confident and daring.
Playing age:	20s.
Act 1, Sce 3:	Imprisoned by Tamburlaine, Callapine convinces his keeper Almeda to release him. He does this by painting a poetic vision of the life that awaits them.

CALLAPINE:

By Cairo runs to Alexandria bay
Darote's stream, wherein at anchor lies
A Turkish galley of my royal fleet,
Waiting my coming to the river side,
Hoping by some means I shall be released,
Which when I come aboard will hoist up sail,
And soon put forth into the Terrene sea,
Where 'twixt the isles of Cyprus and of Crete,
We quickly may in Turkish seas arrive.
Then shalt thou see a hundred kings and more
Upon their knees all bid me welcome home.
Amongst so many crowns of burnished gold,
Choose which thou wilt, all are at thy command;
A thousand galleys manned with Christian slaves
I freely give thee, which shall cut the straits
And bring armadoes from the coasts of Spain,
Fraughted° with gold of rich America;
The Grecian virgins shall attend on thee,
Skilful in music and in amorous lays,°
As fair as was Pygmalion's ivory girl,
Or lovely Iö metamorphosed.
With naked negroes shall thy coach be drawn,
And as thou rid'st in triumph through the streets,
The pavement underneath thy chariot wheels
With Turkey carpets shall be covered,
And cloth of arras hung about the walls,

Fit objects for thy princely eye to pierce.
A hundred bassoes° clothed in crimson silk
Shall ride before thee on Barbarian steeds,
And, when thou goest, a golden canopy
Enchased° with precious stones, which shine as bright
As that fair veil that covers all the world
When Phoebus leaping from his hemisphere
Descendeth downward to th' Antipodes.
And more than this, for all I cannot tell.

fraughted: laden. *lays*: songs, tunes. *bassoes*: generals. *enchased*: decorated.

HENRY VI, PART TWO
by William Shakespeare

Character:	Eleanor, Duchess of Gloucester, female. Clever, ambitious, driven, and scheming.
Playing age:	30s – 40s.
Act 2, Sce 4:	Ambitious that her husband, The Duke of Gloucester, should one day be king (and Eleanor queen) she conspired with occultists to learn of King Henry's fate. Caught and sentenced to banishment, she is paraded through the streets and openly mocked. She wears a white sheet proclaiming the offenses for which she has been found guilty. She addresses her husband.

ELEANOR:

Ah, Gloucester, teach me to forget myself!
For whilst I think I am thy married wife
And thou a prince, protector of this land,
Methinks I should not thus be led along,
Mailed up in shame, with papers on my back,
And followed with a rabble that rejoice
To see my tears and hear my deep-fet groans.
The ruthless flint doth cut my tender feet,
And when I start,° the envious people laugh
And bid me be advised how I tread.
Ah, Humphrey, can I bear this shameful yoke?
Trow'st° thou that e'er I'll look upon the world
Or count them happy that enjoy the sun?
No; dark shall be my light and night my day;
To think upon my pomp shall be my hell.
Sometime I'll say I am Duke Humphrey's wife,
And he a prince and ruler of the land;
Yet so he ruled and such a prince he was
As he stood by whilst I, his forlorn duchess,
Was made a wonder and a pointing-stock°
To every idle rascal follower.
But be thou mild and blush not at my shame,

Martin Jago

Nor stir at nothing till the axe of death
Hang over thee, as sure it shortly will;
For Suffolk, he that can do all in all
With her° that hateth thee and hates us all,
And York and impious Beaufort, that false priest,
Have all limed° bushes to betray thy wings,
And fly thou how thou canst, they'll tangle thee:
But fear not thou until thy foot be snared,
Nor never seek prevention of thy foes.

start: flinch. ***trow'st:*** believe. ***point-stock:*** one derided in the
street. her: i.e. Margaret. ***limed:*** i.e. refers to the practice of
'liming' trees with a sticky lime-based substance to trap birds.

TITUS ANDRONICUS
by William Shakespeare

Character:	Titus, male. A great warrior, battle-hardened and battle-worn, staunch, uncompromising, and proud. A stickler for honor and the rule of law. A military man through and through.
Playing age:	60s.
Act 3, Sce 1:	Titus, his two sons sentenced to death, pleads with the judges for mercy. He throws himself to the ground offering the earth his tears rather than his sons' blood. His pleas are ignored. The judges exit.

TITUS ANDRONICUS:
Hear me, grave fathers, noble tribunes, stay.
For pity of mine age, whose youth was spent
In dangerous wars, whilst you securely slept;
For all my blood in Rome's great quarrel shed;
For all the frosty nights that I have watched,
And for these bitter tears which now you see
Filling the aged wrinkles in my cheeks;
Be pitiful to my condemned sons,
Whose souls are not corrupted as 'tis thought.
For two and twenty sons I never wept,
Because they died in honour's lofty bed.

[Titus lies on the ground. The judges pass him.]

For these two, tribunes, in the dust I write
My heart's deep languor° and my soul's sad tears:
Let my tears stanch° the earth's dry appetite;
My sons' sweet blood will make it shame and blush.

[Exit all but Titus.]

O earth, I will befriend thee more with rain
That shall distil from these two ancient urns°
Than youthful April shall with all his showers.

In summer's drought I'll drop upon thee still;
In winter with warm tears I'll melt the snow
And keep eternal springtime on thy face,
So thou refuse to drink my dear sons' blood.

O reverend tribunes, O gentle, aged men,
Unbind my sons, reverse the doom of death
And let me say, that never wept before,
My tears are now prevailing° orators.

languor: grief. *stanch*: satisfy. *urns*: eyes. *prevailing*: eloquent, compelling.

TITUS ANDRONICUS
by William Shakespeare

Character:	Aaron the Moor, male. Brutal, ruthless, and intelligent.
Playing age:	30s – 50.
Act 5, Sce 1:	Aaron has been captured with his infant son. He is being made to ascend a ladder from which he believes he will be hanged while Lucius threatens to kill the infant. In a desperate bid to save them both Aaron bargains with Lucius, letting it be known that if he dies, so too will all the secrets he bears.

AARON:

Touch not the boy, he is of royal blood.
Lucius, save the child
And bear it from me to the Empress.
If thou do this, I'll show thee wondrous things
That highly may advantage thee to hear;
If thou wilt not, befall what may befall,
I'll speak no more but 'Vengeance rot you all!'

'Twill vex thy soul to hear what I shall speak;
For I must talk of murders, rapes, and massacres,
Acts of black night, abominable deeds,
Complots° of mischief, treason, villainies,
Ruthful° to hear, yet piteously performed;°
And this shall all be buried by my death
Unless thou swear to me my child shall live.

Swear that he shall, and then I will begin.
Yet, for I know thou art religious
And hast a thing within thee called conscience,
With twenty popish° tricks and ceremonies,
Which I have seen thee careful to observe,
Therefore I urge thy oath. For that I know
An idiot holds his bauble° for a god,
And keeps the oath which by that god he swears,

---

42   Martin Jago

To that I'll urge him. Therefore thou shalt vow
By that same god, what god soe'er it be
That thou adorest and hast in reverence,
To save my boy, to nourish and bring him up;
Or else I will discover nought to thee.

complots: conspiracies. ***ruthful***: sorrowful. ***piteously performed***: done without pity. ***popish***: Catholic. ***bauble***: a doll, a fool's stick.

RICHARD III

by William Shakespeare

Character:	George, Duke of Clarence, male. Trusting, eloquent, gullible.
Playing age:	20s – 30s.
Act 1, Sce 4:	Shortly before his murder, in which he is first stabbed and later drowned in a vat of wine, Clarence awakes in his cell and recalls a vivid and portentous dream.

CLARENCE:
O, I have passed a miserable night,
So full of fearful dreams, of ugly sights,
That as I am a Christian faithful man,
I would not spend another such a night
Though 'twere to buy a world of happy days,
So full of dismal terror was the time.

Methoughts that I had broken from the Tower
And was embarked to cross the Burgundy,
And in my company my brother Gloucester,
Who from my cabin tempted me to walk
Upon the hatches. Thence we looked toward England
And cited up° a thousand heavy times,
During the wars of York and Lancaster,
That had befall'n us. As we paced along
Upon the giddy footing of the hatches,
Methought that Gloucester stumbled, and in falling
Struck me, that thought to stay him, overboard
Into the tumbling billows of the main.
O Lord, methought what pain it was to drown,
What dreadful noise of waters in mine ears,
What sights of ugly death within mine eyes!
Methoughts I saw a thousand fearful wrecks,
A thousand men that fishes gnawed upon;
Wedges of gold, great anchors, heaps of pearl,
Inestimable stones, unvalued° jewels,

All scattered in the bottom of the sea;
Some lay in dead men's skulls, and in the holes
Where eyes did once inhabit, there were crept,
As 'twere in scorn of eyes, reflecting gems,
That wooed the slimy bottom of the deep
And mocked the dead bones that lay scattered by.

cited up: recalled. ***unvalued***: priceless.

EDWARD II
by Christopher Marlowe

Character:	Edward, male. A king who is obstinate and licentious. His status, eloquence, manner, and circumstances provide obvious parallels with Richard II (two Richard monologues follow the Edward speeches in this collection).
Playing age:	30s – 40s.
Act 5, Sce 1:	Imprisoned in Kenilworth Castle, Edward laments his overthrow. Leicester, The Bishop of Winchester, and Trussell are present. The Bishop and Trussell press for Edward to resign his crown.

EDWARD:

Leicester, if gentle words might comfort me,
Thy speeches long ago had eased my sorrows,
For kind and loving hast thou always been.
The griefs of private men are soon allayed;
But not of kings. The forest deer, being struck,
Runs to an herb that closeth up the wounds;
But when the imperial lion's flesh is gored,
He rends and tears it with his wrathful paw,
And highly scorning that the lowly earth
Should drink his blood, mounts up into the air:
And so it fares with me, whose dauntless mind
Th' ambitious Mortimer would seek to curb,
And that unnatural queen, false Isabel,
That thus hath pent and mewed me in a prison
For such outrageous passions cloy my soul,
As with the wings of rancour and disdain
Full often am I soaring up to heaven,
To plain me to the gods against them both.
But when I call to mind I am a king,
Methinks I should revenge me of my wrongs
That Mortimer and Isabel have done.
But what are kings, when regiment° is gone,
But perfect shadows in a sunshine day?

My nobles rule; I bear the name of king;
I wear the crown; but am controlled by them,
By Mortimer, and my unconstant queen,
Who spots my nuptial bed with infamy;
Whilst I am lodged within this cave of care,
Where sorrow at my elbow still attends,
To company my heart with sad laments,
That bleeds within me for this strange exchange.
But tell me, must I now resign my crown,
To make usurping Mortimer a king?

regiment: rule.

EDWARD II

by Christopher Marlowe

Character:	Edward, male. A king who is obstinate and licentious. His status, eloquence, manner, and circumstances provide obvious parallels with Richard II (see the following speech of this collection).
Playing age:	30s – 40s.
Act 5, Sce 1:	Imprisoned in Kenilworth Castle, Edward responds to the demands for him to resign his crown. Leicester, Trussell, and Winchester are present.

EDWARD:

Ah Leicester, weigh how hardly I can brook
To lose my crown and kingdom without cause;
To give ambitious Mortimer my right,
That like a mountain overwhelms my bliss,
In which extreme my mind here murdered is!
But what the heavens appoint, I must obey.
Here, take my crown; the life of Edward too;

[Taking off the crown.]

Two kings in England cannot reign at once.
But stay awhile, let me be king till night
That I may gaze upon this glittering crown;
So shall my eyes receive their last content,
My head, the latest honour due to it,
And jointly both yield up their wished right.
Continue ever, thou celestial sun;
Let never silent night possess this clime;
Stand still you watches of the element;
All times and seasons rest you at a stay,
That Edward may be still fair England's king!
But day's bright beam doth vanish fast away,
And needs I must resign my wished crown.
Inhuman creatures, nursed with tiger's milk,

Why gape you for your sovereign's overthrow?
My diadem, I mean, and guiltless life.
See, monsters, see. I'll wear my crown again!

[He puts on the crown.]

What, fear you not the fury of your king?
But, hapless Edward, thou art fondly° led;
They pass° not for thy frowns as late they did,
But seek to make a new-elected king;
Which fills my mind with strange despairing thoughts,
Which thoughts are martyred with endless torments,
And in this torment comfort find I none,
But that I feel the crown upon my head;
And therefore let me wear it yet a while.

fondly: foolishly, stupidly. ***pass***: care.

RICHARD II

by William Shakespeare

Character:	King Richard II, male. Young, willful, and unyielding. Given to flights poetic speech, he has a great facility for soaring rhetoric and eloquence. Richard believes in the divine rights of kings and enjoys the trappings of his position. He can be wasteful and immature and is detached from the common man.
Playing age:	20s – 30s.
Act 5, Sce 5:	Overthrown and imprisoned in Pomfret Castle, Richard contemplates his changed fortunes.

RICHARD:

I have been studying how I may compare
This prison where I live unto the world,
And for because the world is populous
And here is not a creature but myself,
I cannot do it. Yet I'll hammer° it out.
My brain I'll prove the female to my soul,
My soul the father; and these two beget
A generation of still-breeding° thoughts,
And these same thoughts people this little world,
In humours like the people of this world,
For no thought is contented. The better sort,
As thoughts of things divine, are intermixed
With scruples° and do set the word itself
Against the word,
As thus: 'Come, little ones,' and then again,
'It is as hard to come as for a camel
To thread the postern of a small needle's eye.'
Thoughts tending to ambition, they do plot
Unlikely wonders: how these vain weak nails
May tear a passage through the flinty ribs
Of this hard world, my ragged° prison walls,
And for they cannot, die in their own pride.
Thoughts tending to content flatter themselves

That they are not the first of fortune's slaves,
Nor shall not be the last; like silly beggars
Who sitting in the stocks refuge their shame,
That many have and others must sit there;
And in this thought they find a kind of ease,
Bearing their own misfortunes on the back
Of such as have before endured the like.
Thus play I in one person many people,
And none contented. Sometimes am I king;
Then treasons make me wish myself a beggar,
And so I am. Then crushing penury
Persuades me I was better when a king;
Then am I kinged again: and by and by
Think that I am unkinged by Bolingbroke,
And straight am nothing. But whate'er I be,
Nor I, nor any man that but man is,
With nothing shall be pleased, till he be eased
With being nothing.

hammer: work. **still-breeding:** continually-breeding. **scruples:** doubts. **ragged:** rugged.

RICHARD II

by William Shakespeare

Character:	King Richard II, male.
Playing age:	20s – 30s.
Act 5, Sce 5:	Overthrown and imprisoned in Pomfret Castle, Richard's soliloquy, a continuation of the previous speech, focuses on his fortunes and the human condition.

RICHARD:
Music do I hear?

[Music plays.]

Ha, ha! Keep time. How sour sweet music is,
When time is broke and no proportion kept!
So is it in the music of men's lives.
And here have I the daintiness of ear
To check° time broke in a disordered string;
But for the concord° of my state and time
Had not an ear to hear my true time broke.
I wasted time, and now doth time waste me;
For now hath time made me his numbering clock:
My thoughts are minutes; and with sighs they jar
Their watches on unto mine eyes, the outward watch,
Whereto my finger, like a dial's point,
Is pointing still,° in cleansing them from tears.
Now sir, the sound that tells what hour it is
Are clamorous groans, which strike upon my heart,
Which is the bell. So sighs and tears and groans
Show minutes, times, and hours; but my time
Runs posting° on in Bolingbroke's proud joy,
While I stand fooling here, his Jack o' the clock.
This music mads me. Let it sound no more;
For though it have holp° madmen to their wits,
In me it seems it will make wise men mad.

Martin Jago

Yet blessing on his heart that gives it me!
For 'tis a sign of love; and love to Richard
Is a strange brooch° in this all-hating world.

check: scold. ***concord:*** harmony. ***still:*** continually. ***posting:*** hurrying. ***holp:*** helped. ***a strange brooch:*** a rare jewel.

THE MERCHANT OF VENICE
by William Shakespeare

Character:	Shylock, male. A Jewish merchant. Mistreated, wronged, ruthless, intelligent, eloquent.
Playing age:	50-60s.
Act 4, Sce 1:	Shylock's hatred for Antonio has been shaped by Antonio's anti-Semitism. The pair are now in court, Shylock demanding a pound of Antonio's flesh as stipulated in a contract should Antonio break its terms. Shylock explains that if the debt is not honored, the law is worthless. He never explains his unwillingness to yield in the case.

SHYLOCK:
I have possessed° your grace of what I purpose,
And by our holy Sabbath have I sworn
To have the due and forfeit of my bond.
If you deny it, let the danger° light
Upon your charter and your city's freedom.
You'll ask me why I rather choose to have
A weight of carrion flesh than to receive
Three thousand ducats. I'll not answer that
But say it is my humour:° is it answered?
What if my house be troubled with a rat
And I be pleased to give ten thousand ducats
To have it baned?° What, are you answered yet?
Some men there are love not a gaping pig;
Some that are mad if they behold a cat;
And others when the bagpipe sings i' th' nose,
Cannot contain their urine; for affection,°
Mistress of passion, sways it to the mood
Of what it likes or loathes. Now, for your answer:
As there is no firm reason to be rendered
Why he cannot abide a gaping pig;
Why he, a harmless necessary cat;
Why he, a woollen bagpipe, but of force
Must yield to such inevitable shame

Martin Jago

As to offend, himself being offended;
So can I give no reason, nor I will not,
More than a lodged° hate and a certain loathing
I bear Antonio, that I follow thus
A losing suit against him. Are you answered?

possessed: informed. **danger**: harm. **humour**: mood. **baned**: poisoned.
affection: compulsion. **lodged**: firm, strong.

ANTONIO'S REVENGE
by John Marston

Character:	Maria, female. A matron. Humble, honest, and plain-talking.
Playing age:	40s – 60s.
Act 4, Sce 3:	Mellida has fled and died of a broken heart, believing her lover, Maria's son, to be dead. He is not. Maria returns to court and reports her mistress' death.

MARIA:

O piteous end of love! O too, too rude hand
Of unrespective° death! Alas, sweet maid!
The beauty of admired creation,
The life of modest unmixed purity,
Our sex's glory—dead!
Being laid upon her bed, she grasped my hand,
And kissing it, spake thus: "Thou very poor,
Why dost not weep? The jewel of thy brow,
The rich adornment that enchased° thy breast,
Is lost: thy son, my love, is lost, is dead.
And do I live to say Antonio's dead?
And have I lived to see his virtues blurred
With guiltless blots?° O world, thou art too subtle
For honest natures to converse withal,
Therefore I'll leave thee; farewell, mart° of woe,
I fly to clip my love, Antonio!"
With that her head sunk down upon her breast;
Her cheek changed earth,° her senses slept in rest,
Until my fool, that pressed unto the bed,
Screeched out so loud that he brought back her soul,
Called her again, that her bright eyes gan ope,°
And stared upon him. He, audacious fool,
Dared kiss her hand, wished her "soft rest, loved bride;"
She fumbled out, "thanks, good;" and so she died.

unrespective: unrespecting. *enchased*: encased, held in. *guiltless blots*: accused crimes not committed. *mart*: valley. *changed earth*: died. *gan ope*: began to open.

ANTONIO'S REVENGE
by John Marston

Character:	Sir Geoffrey Balurdo, male. A foolish courtier with a love of puns and song.
Playing age:	30s – 60s.
Act 5, Sce 2:	Balurdo escapes from his prison cell.

BALURDO:

Ho! Who's above there? Ho! A murrain° on all proverbs: They say hunger breaks through stone walls, but I am as gaunt as lean-ribbed famine, yet I can burst through no stone walls. O now, Sir Geoffrey, show thy valour, break prison and be hanged.

[He climbs from the dungeon.]

Nor shall the darkest nook of hell contain
The discontented Sir Balurdo's ghost.

Well, I am out well; I have put off the prison to put on the rope.° O poor shotten herring,° what a pickle art thou in! O hunger, how thou domineerest° in my guts! O for a fat leg of ewe mutton in stewed broth, or drunken song to feed on! I could belch rarely, for I am all wind. O cold, cold, cold, cold, cold! O poor knight! O poor Sir Geoffrey, sing like an unicorn before thou dost dip thy horn in the water of death. O cold, O sing, O cold, O poor Sir Geoffrey, sing, sing!

[He sings.]

-

murrain: plague. **put...rope**: his escape is punishable by hanging. **shotten herring**: dispirited person. **domineerest**: dominates.

MEASURE FOR MEASURE
by William Shakespeare

Character:	Duke Vincentio of Vienna, male. Committed more to study than leadership. A benevolent ruler during whose reign the laws have been disregarded.
Playing age:	30s – 50s.
Act 3, Sce 1:	Disguised as a friar the Duke visits the condemned Claudio in prison and advises him to prepare for the worst.

DUKE VINCENTIO:

Be absolute° for death; either death or life
Shall thereby be the sweeter. Reason thus with life:
If I do lose thee, I do lose a thing
That none but fools would keep: a breath thou art,
Servile to all the skyey influences,
That dost this habitation, where thou keep'st,°
Hourly afflict: merely,° thou art death's fool;
For him thou labour'st by thy flight to shun
And yet runn'st toward him still.° Thou art not noble;
For all the accommodations° that thou bear'st
Are nursed by baseness. Thou'rt by no means valiant;
For thou dost fear the soft and tender fork°
Of a poor worm.° Thy best of rest is sleep,
And that thou oft provok'st;° yet grossly fear'st
Thy death, which is no more. Thou art not thyself;°
For thou exist'st on many a thousand grains
That issue out of dust. Happy thou art not;
For what thou hast not, still thou striv'st to get,
And what thou hast, forget'st. Thou art not certain;°
For thy complexion° shifts to strange effects,
After the moon. If thou art rich, thou'rt poor;
For, like an ass whose back with ingots bows,
Thou bear's thy heavy riches but a journey,
And death unloads thee. Friend hast thou none;
For thine own bowels,° which do call thee sire,
The mere effusion of thy proper loins,°

Do curse the gout, serpigo,° and the rheum,°
For ending thee no sooner. Thou hast nor youth nor age,
But, as it were, an after-dinner's sleep,
Dreaming on both; for all thy blessed youth
Becomes as aged, and doth beg the alms
Of palsied eld;° and when thou art old and rich,
Thou hast neither heat,° affection, limb,° nor beauty,
To make thy riches pleasant. What's yet in this
That bears the name of life? Yet in this life
Lie hid more thousand deaths: yet death we fear,
That makes these odds° all even.

absolute: prepared, resolved. *keep'st*: live. *merely*: completely. *still*: always. *accommodations*: comforts. *fork*: forked tongue. *worm*: snake. *provok'st*: make use of. *thyself*: self-contained. *certain*: firm, stable. *complexion*: mood. *bowels*: progeny. *the mere...loins*: were self-produced. *serpigo*: ringworm. *rheum*: mucous. *eld*: elders. *heat*: passion. *limb*: strength. *odds*: peculiarities.

MEASURE FOR MEASURE
by William Shakespeare

Character: Claudio, male. A young, immature man of Vienna.
Playing age: 20s – 30s.
Act 3, Sce 1:   A condemned man, Claudio paints a horrid picture
                 of death before pleading with his sister that she
                 accepts the bargain Angelo has made by trading her
                 virginity for his freedom.

CLAUDIO:
Ay, but to die, and go we know not where;
To lie in cold obstruction° and to rot;
This sensible warm motion to become
A kneaded clod; and the delighted spirit
To bathe in fiery floods, or to reside
In thrilling° region of thick-ribbed ice;
To be imprisoned in the viewless winds,
And blown with restless violence round about
The pendent° world; or to be worse than worst
Of those that lawless and incertain thought
Imagine howling: 'tis too horrible!
The weariest and most loathed worldly life
That age, ache, penury and imprisonment
Can lay on nature is a paradise
To what we fear of death.

Sweet sister, let me live:
What sin you do to save a brother's life,
Nature dispenses with the deed so far
That it becomes a virtue.

obstruction: condition, i.e. state of being dead. **thrilling**: freezing.
pendent: suspended in space.

MEASURE FOR MEASURE
by William Shakespeare

Character:	Isabella, female. A young virginal woman who is strictly moralist, and perhaps a little self-righteous. She is a devout Christian who wishes to be a nun.
Playing age:	20s – 30s.
Act 3, Sce 1:	Visiting her brother in prison the day before he is due to die, Isabella reveals that de facto ruler Angelo has proposed his freedom for her virginity. Sure her brother wouldn't condone such a proposition, she is outraged to learn the opposite is true.

ISABELLA:

What says my brother? O you beast! Alas!
O faithless coward! O dishonest wretch!
Wilt thou be made a man° out of my vice?
Is't not a kind of incest, to take life
From thine own sister's shame? What should I think?
Heaven shield° my mother played my father fair!
For such a warped slip of wilderness
Ne'er issued from his blood. Take my defiance!
Die, perish! Might but my bending down
Reprieve thee from thy fate, it should proceed:
I'll pray a thousand prayers for thy death,
No word to save thee.

O, fie, fie, fie!
Thy sin's not accidental, but a trade.
Mercy to thee would prove itself a bawd:
'Tis best thou diest quickly.

made a man: i.e. live. ***shield***: forbid.

MEASURE FOR MEASURE
by William Shakespeare

Character:	Pompey, male. A bawdy fellow with the gift of the gab. A sometime pimp, sometime barman for Mistress Overdone.
Playing age:	30s – 60s.
Act 4, Sce 3:	In prison, Pompey says he is as well acquainted with the place as he is with Mistress Overdone's brothel and is amused to see they share many of the same 'clients.'

POMPEY:

I am as well acquainted here as I was in our house of profession. One would think it were Mistress Overdone's own house, for here be many of her old customers. First, here's young Master Rash; he's in for a commodity of brown paper and old ginger, nine score and seventeen pounds; of which he made five marks, ready money. Marry, then ginger was not much in request, for the old women were all dead. Then is there here one Master Caper, at the suit of Master Threepile the mercer,° for some four suits of peach-coloured satin, which now peaches° him a beggar. Then have we here young Dizzy, and young Master Deepvow, and Master Copperspur, and Master Starve-lackey the rapier and dagger man, and young Drophair that killed lusty Pudding, and Master Forthlight the tilter°, and brave Master Shoetie the great traveller, and wild Half-can that stabbed Pots, and I think forty more, all great doers in our trade, and are now 'for the Lord's sake.'

mercer: fabric trader. *peaches*: impeaches. *tilter*: fencer.

JACOBEAN AGE (1603 – 1625)

A WOMAN KILLED WITH KINDNESS
by Thomas Heywood

Character:	Sir Charles Mountford, male. Unfortunate, hot-headed, and impulsive.
Playing age:	30s – 50s.
Act 4, Sce 1:	This is the second time Sir Charles has ended up in prison. He laments his circumstances, cursing his friends for their disloyalty only to make a volte face when the keeper informs him that he is to be released.

SIR CHARLES:

Of all on the earth's face most miserable,
Breathe in the hellish dungeon thy laments.
Thus like a slave ragged, like a felon gyved,°
That hurls thee headlong to this base estate.
O unkind° uncle! O my friends ingrate!
Unthankful kinsmen! Mountfords all too base!
To let thy name lie fettered in disgrace!
A thousand deaths here in this grave I die:
Fear, hunger, sorrow, cold: all threat my death,
And join together to deprive my breath.
But that which most torments me, my dear sister
Hath left to visit me, and from my friends
Hath brought no hopeful answer; therefore I
Divine they will not help my misery.
If it be so, shame, scandal and contempt
Attend their covetous thoughts, need make their graves.
Usurers they live, and may they die like slaves.

O! "Your appeal is stayed; Go freely to
Your house or where you please"?

Thou grumblest out the sweetest music to me
That ever organ played. Is this a dream?
Or do my waking senses apprehend
The pleasing taste of these applausive° news?

Slave that I was to wrong such honest friends,
My loving kinsmen and my near allies.
Tongue, I will bite thee for the scandal breath
Against such faithful kinsmen. They are all
Composed of pity and compassion,
Of melting charity, and of moving ruth.°
That which I spake before was in my rage;
They are my friends, the mirrors of this age,
Bounteous and free. The noble Mountfords' race
Ne'er bred a covetous thought or humour° base.

gyved: shackled. **unkind**: cruel. **applausive**: welcome. **ruth**: compassion. **humour**: disposition.

THE HONEST WHORE, PART TWO
by Thomas Dekker

Character:	A Master of Bridewell prison, male. Proud, honest, and earthy.
Playing age:	40s – 50s.
Act 5, Sce 2:	Bridewell was variously a prison, madhouse, and hospital. The Master extols its virtues with great respect and faith in the institution's powers of correction.

MASTER:
Here Providence and Charity play such parts,
The house is like a very school of arts,
For when our soldiers like ships driven from sea,
With ribs all broken, and with tattered sides,
Cast anchor here again, their ragged backs
How often do we cover! That, like men,
They may be sent to their own homes again.
All here are but one swarm of bees, and strive
To bring with wearied thighs honey to the hive.
The sturdy° beggar, and the lazy loon,
Gets here hard hands° or laced correction.°
The vagabond grows stayed, and learns to 'bey,
The drone° is beaten well, and sent away.
As other prisons are, some for the thief,
Some, by which undone credit gets relief
From bridled debtors; others for the poor,
So this is for the bawd, the rogue, and whore.

Nor is it seen
That the whip draws blood here to cool the spleen°
Of any rugged bencher:° nor does offence
Feel smart,° or spiteful, or rash° evidence:
But pregnant° testimony forth must stand,
Ere justice leave them in the beadle's° hand,
As iron, on the anvil are they laid,
Not to take blows alone, but to be made

And fashioned to some charitable use,
Thus wholsom'st laws spring from the worst abuse.

---

sturdy: persistent, continual. *hard hands*: put to work. *laced correction*: restrained with ropes. *drone*: an idler. *spleen*: anger. *bencher*: a judge, member of court. *smart*: cruel, painful. *rash*: hasty. *pregnant*: evident. *beadle*: public whipper.

IF YOU KNOW NOT ME, YOU KNOW NOBODY
by Thomas Heywood

Character:	Constable of the Tower of London, male; stubborn and unyielding.
Playing age:	Any age but probably 40s – 60s.
Act 2, Sce 4:	The Constable has taken 'care' of the royal princess but refuses to give her special treatment, intending to carry out his duties to the letter of the law. Despite her royal status he finds his Protestant prisoner contemptible.

CONSTABLE:
"Only the casements° of her window ope,°
Whereby she may receive fresh, gladsome air?"

Oh! You preach well to deaf men: no, not I.
So letters may fly in; I'll none of that.
She is my prisoner; and if I durst,°
But that my warrant is not yet so strict,
I'd lay her in a dungeon, where her eyes
Should not have light to read her prayer book.
So would I danger both soul and body,
'Cause she an alien is to us Catholics:
Her bed should be all snakes, her rest despair:
Torture should make her curse her faithless prayer.

This base groom flouts me. Oh! This frets° my heart:
These knaves will jet° upon their privilege.
But yet I'll vex her: I have found the means.
I'll have my cooks to dress my meat with hers,
And every officer my men shall match.
Oh! That I could drain her dear heart's blood.
Oh! It would feed me—do my soul much good.

casements: hinged windows. **ope**: open. **durst**: dare. **frets**: troubles, bothers. **jet**: throw, i.e. exercise influence.

THE REVENGER'S TRAGEDY
by Thomas Middleton

Character: Duchess, female. A scheming, lustful cougar, hell-
              bent on sex and power.
Playing age: 40s – 50s.
Act 1, Sce 2: When everyone has left the court the Duchess
              remains. She is angry that the Duke has failed to
              acquit her (guilty) son of rape. When Spurio, the
              Duke's bastard son enters, the Duchess turns her
              lustful intentions towards him.

DUCHESS:
Wast ever known step-duchess was so mild
And calm as I? Some now would plot his death
With easy doctors,° those loose-living men,
And make his withered grace fall to his grave
And keep church better.°
Some second wife would do this, and dispatch
Her double-loathed lord at meat and sleep.
Indeed, 'tis true an old man's twice a child.
Mine cannot speak; one of his single words
Would quite have freed my youngest, dearest son
From death or durance,° and have made him walk
With a bold foot upon the thorny law,
Whose prickles should bow under him: but 'tis not,
And therefore wedlock, faith, shall be forgot.
I'll kill him in his forehead;° hate there feed:
That wound is deepest tho' it never bleed.

[Spurio enters.]

And here comes he whom my heart points unto,
His bastard son, but my love's true-begot.
Many a wealthy letter have I sent him,
Swelled up with jewels, and the timorous man
Is yet but coldly kind;
That jewel's mine that quivers in his ear,

Mocking his master's chillness and vain fear.
H'as spied me now.

easy doctors: corrupt doctors. *keep church better*: i.e. since he will be buried there. *durance*: imprisonment. *kill him in his forehead*: make him a cuckold.

THE REVENGER'S TRAGEDY
by Thomas Middleton

Character:	Junior, male. Remorseless, arrogant, and lecherous.
Playing age:	20s.
Act 3, Sce 4:	Junior is in prison for rape but awaits impatiently some scheme from his brothers that will free him.

JUNIOR:
Nothing but paper comforts?
I looked for my delivery° before this
Had they been worth their oaths. Prithee be from us.

[Exit the Keeper.]

Now what say you, forsooth? Speak out, I pray.

[Opens and reads the letter.]

"Brother be of good cheer."
'Slud, it begins like a whore with good cheer!
"Thou shalt not be long a prisoner."
Not five and thirty year like a bankrout,° I think so.
"We have thought upon a device to get thee out by a trick."
By a trick! Pox a' your trick and it be so long a-playing!
"And so rest comforted, be merry and expect it suddenly."
Be merry, hang merry, draw and quarter merry, I'll be mad!
Is't not strange that a man should lie in° a whole month for a
woman? Well, we shall see how sudden our brothers will be in
their promise. I must expect still a trick! I shall not be long a
prisoner! *[Enter Keeper.]* How now, what news?

delivery: freedom. *bankrout*: an imprisoned, bankrupt person. *lie in*:
serve time in prison.

THE WINTER'S TALE
by William Shakespeare

Character:	Hermione, female. A queen, a mother, and a wife. She stands trial having been falsely accused of adultery by her husband. She is dignified and poised. A strong women who has been wronged.
Playing age:	20s – 30s.
Act 3, Sce 2:	Accused of adultery, Hermione speaks with dignity in court. She explains pleading not guilty is pointless because Leontes has already decided she is guilty.

HERMIONE:
Since what I am to say must be but that
Which contradicts my accusation and
The testimony on my part no other
But what comes from myself, it shall scarce boot° me
To say 'not guilty:' mine integrity
Being counted falsehood, shall, as I express it,
Be so received. But thus: if powers divine
Behold our human actions, as they do,
I doubt not then but innocence shall make
False accusation blush and tyranny
Tremble at patience. You, my lord, best know,
Who least will seem to do so, my past life
Hath been as continent,° as chaste, as true,
As I am now unhappy; which is more
Than history° can pattern, though devised
And played to take spectators. For behold me
A fellow of the royal bed, which owe°
A moiety° of the throne, a great king's daughter,
The mother to a hopeful prince, here standing
To prate and talk for life and honour 'fore
Who please to come and hear. For life, I prize it
As I weigh grief, which I would spare:° for honour,
'Tis a derivative from me to mine,
And only that I stand for. I appeal
To your own conscience, sir, before Polixenes

Came to your court, how I was in your grace,
How merited to be so; since he came,
With what encounter° so uncurrent I
Have strained to appear thus: if one jot beyond
The bound of honour, or in act or will
That way inclining, hardened be the hearts
Of all that hear me, and my near'st of kin
Cry fie upon my grave!

---

boot: help. *continent*: self-restrained. *history*: a history play. *owe*: own. *moiety*: equal share. *spare*: avoid. *encounter*: behavior.

THE WINTER'S TALE
by William Shakespeare

Character:	Hermione, female. A queen, a mother, and a wife. She stands trial having been falsely accused of adultery by her husband. She is dignified and poised. A strong women who has been wronged.
Playing age:	Late 20s – 30s.
Act 3, Sce 2:	Hermione explains with dignity that she won't be cowed by threats. She cares for her honor more than death and having been dishonored by unfair accusations there is no satisfaction in life.

HERMIONE:

Sir, spare your threats:
The bug which you would fright me with I seek.
To me can life be no commodity:
The crown and comfort of my life, your favour,
I do give° lost; for I do feel it gone,
But know not how it went. My second joy
And first-fruits of my body, from his presence
I am barred, like one infectious. My third comfort
Starred° most unluckily, is from my breast,
The innocent milk in its most innocent mouth,
Haled° out to murder: myself on every post
Proclaimed a strumpet: with immodest hatred
The child-bed privilege denied, which 'longs
To women of all fashion; lastly, hurried
Here to this place, i' the open air, before
I have got strength of limit. Now, my liege,
Tell me what blessings I have here alive,
That I should fear to die? Therefore proceed.
But yet hear this: mistake me not; no life,
I prize it not a straw,° but for mine honour,
Which I would free, if I shall be condemned
Upon surmises, all proofs sleeping else
But what your jealousies awake, I tell you
'Tis rigor and not law. Your honours all,

I do refer me to the oracle:
Apollo be my judge!

give: consider. ***starred***: born under a star. ***hale***: hauled. *a straw*: a jot,
a trifle.

Martin Jago

THE WINTER'S TALE
by William Shakespeare

Character:	Paulina, female. A noblewoman who is fiercely loyal to Hermione, defending her honor and attacking Leontes.
Playing age:	30s – 40s.
Act 3, Sce 2:	News arrives that Hermione's son has died. She collapses and is carried from the court. Paulina returns a short while later, attacking Leontes, revealing that Hermione has also died, and blaming him for her death.

PAULINA:
What studied° torments, tyrant, hast for me?
What wheels, racks, fires? What flaying, boiling,
In leads or oils? What old or newer torture
Must I receive, whose every word deserves
To taste of thy most worst? Thy tyranny
Together working with thy jealousies,
Fancies° too weak for boys, too green and idle
For girls of nine. O, think what they have done
And then run mad indeed, stark mad! For all
Thy bygone fooleries were but spices of it.
That thou betrayedst Polixenes, 'twas nothing;
That did but show thee, of a fool, inconstant
And damnable ingrateful: nor was't much,
Thou wouldst have poisoned good Camillo's honour,
To have him kill a king: poor trespasses,
More monstrous standing by: whereof I reckon
The casting forth to crows thy baby-daughter
To be or none or little; though a devil
Would have shed water out of fire ere done't:
Nor is't directly laid to thee, the death
Of the young prince, whose honourable thoughts,
Thoughts high for one so tender, cleft the heart
That could conceive a gross and foolish sire
Blemished his gracious dam: this is not, no,

Laid to thy answer: but the last - o lords,
When I have said,° cry woe! The queen, the queen,
The sweet'st, dear'st creature's dead! And vengeance for't
Not dropped down yet.

studied: well-planned. *fancies*: imaginings. **when I have said**: when I have finished speaking.

Martin Jago

CYMBERLINE

by William Shakespeare

Character:	Posthumus, male. A gentleman of low birth who is educated, courteous, and impulsive.
Playing age:	20s.
Act 5, Sce 4:	Posthumus welcomes imprisonment since he hopes it serves, in part, to help atone for the murder of Imogen, which he ordered when he believed she had betrayed their love. He wants to punish himself. In fact, Imogen lives, though Posthumus has yet to discover this.

POSTHUMUS:
Most welcome, bondage! For thou art a way,
I think, to liberty. Yet am I better
Than one that's sick o' th' gout, since he had rather
Groan so in perpetuity than be cured
By th' sure physician Death, who is the key
T' unbar these locks. My conscience, thou art fettered
More than my shanks and wrists; you good gods, give me
The penitent instrument to pick that bolt,
Then, free forever! Is't enough I am sorry?
So children temporal fathers do appease;
Gods are more full of mercy. Must I repent?
I cannot do it better than in gyves,°
Desired more than constrained: to satisfy,°
If of my freedom 'tis the main part, take
No stricter° render of me than my all.
I know you are more clement than vile men,
Who of their broken° debtors take a third,
A sixth, a tenth, letting them thrive again
On their abatement. That's not my desire.
For Imogen's dear life take mine; and though
'Tis not so dear, yet 'tis a life; you coined it.
'Tween man and man they weigh not every stamp;°
Though light, take pieces for the figure's sake:
You rather mine, being yours. And so, great powers,

If you will take this audit,° take this life,
And cancel these cold bonds.° O Imogen!
I'll speak to thee in silence.

[He sleeps.]

---

gyves: shackles. *to satisfy:* to atone. *no stricter:* no less than. *broken:* bankrupt. *'tween man…stamp*: coins with the sovereign's head stamped on them are accepted as legal tender even though they may be lighter i.e. counterfeit. Posthumus is saying that his life is not worth as much as Imogen's but it is everything he has to offer and therefore prays it is accepted in her place. *take this audit:* accept my account. *cancel these cold bonds*: release me from these shackles.

Martin Jago

CYMBERLINE

by William Shakespeare

Character:	Jailer, male. Full of dark irony and gallows humor.
Playing age:	30s – 60s.
Act 5, Sce 4:	The Jailer prepares Posthumus for execution reflecting on the benefits of death.

JAILER:

Come, sir, are you ready for death? Hanging is the word, sir; if you be ready for that, you are well cooked.° A heavy reckoning for you, sir—but the comfort is, you shall be called to no more payments; fear no more tavern bills, which are often the sadness of parting, as the procuring of mirth; you come in faint—for want of meat, depart reeling with too much drink; sorry that you have paid too much, and sorry that you are paid too much; purse and brain both empty; the brain the heavier for being too light, the purse too light, being drawn of heaviness. O, of this contradiction you shall now be quit. O, the charity of a penny cord! It sums up thousands in a trice. You have no true debitor and creditor° but it; of what's past, is, and to come, the discharge. Your neck, sir, is pen, book and counters; so the acquittance follows. Indeed, sir, he that sleeps feels not the toothache. But a man that were to sleep your sleep, and a hangman to help him to bed, I think he would change places with his officer; for look you, sir, you know not which way you shall go.°

---

well cooked: more than ready. **debitor and creditor**: accounts/account book. **you know not...shall go**: i.e. to heaven or hell.

A NEW WONDER, A WOMAN NEVER VEXED
by William Rowley

Character:	Old Foster, male. An honest, principled if not inflexible merchant.
Playing age:	40s – 60s.
Act 4, Sce 2:	Seeking refuge in Ludgate prison, away from his creditors, Old Foster is visited by his estranged son. He rejects him and his offer of help. He also expresses dislike for his own brother, the boy's uncle, whom he believes to be immoral and a bad influence.

OLD FOSTER:
O torment to my soul! What mak'st thou here?
Cannot the picture of my misery
Be drawn and hung out to the eyes of men,
But thou most come to scorn and laugh at it?

Hence from my sight, dissembling° villain, go!
Thine uncle sends° defiance to my woe,
And thou must bring it. Hence, thou basilisk
That kill'st me with mine eyes.° Nay, never kneel;
These scornful mocks more than my woes I feel.

Him and thee I curse;
I'll starve 'fore I eat bread from his purse
Or from thy hand; Out, villain! Tell that cur,
Thy barking uncle, that I lie not here
Upon my bed of riot,° as he did,
Covered with all the villainies which man
Had ever woven; tell him I lie not so—
It was the hand of heaven struck me thus low,
And I do thank it.° Get thee gone, I say,
Or if thou'lt laugh thy fill at my poor state,
Then stay and listen to the prison grate
That yesterday had thousands beg and cry
To get a penny. Oh, my misery!

Upon my curse I charge no nearer come,
I'll be no father to so vile a son.

---

dissembling: deceitful. *sends*: adds. *mine eyes*: my son's eyes, i.e. my flesh and blood. *bed of riot*: prison bed. *and...thank it*: i.e. grateful because my misfortunes weren't caused through personal vice.

THE WHITE DEVIL
by John Webster

Character: Vittoria, female. Passionate, worldly, immediate, and emotional.

Playing age: 20s.

Act 4, Sce 2:   Imprisoned in a 'house of convertities' (a place for reformed prostitutes), Vittoria, has been accused by her lover Brachiano of receiving love letters. Here, she bites back.

VITTORIA:
What have I gained by thee but infamy?
Thou hast stained the spotless honour of my house,
And frighted thence noble society:
Like those, which sick o' th' palsy, and retain
Ill-scenting foxes° 'bout them, are still shunned
By those of choicer nostrils. What do you call this house?
Is this your palace? Did not the judge style it
A house of penitent whores? Who sent me to it?
To this incontinent° college? Is't not you?
Is't not your high preferment? Go, go, brag
How many ladies you have undone, like me.
Fare you well, sir. Let me hear no more of you!
I had a limb corrupted to an ulcer,
But I have cut it off; and now I'll go
Weeping to heaven on crutches. For your gifts,
I will return them all, and I do wish
That I could make you full executor
To all my sins. O that I could toss myself
Into a grave as quickly! For all thou art worth
I'll not shed one tear more—I'll burst first.

---

sick...foxes: a reference to the use of fox to cure palsy. ***incontinent***: unrestrained.

              Martin Jago

HENRY VIII

by William Shakespeare

Character:	Duke of Buckingham, male. Honorable yet quick-tempered. He has a deep loathing of his enemies.
Playing age:	40s – 50s.
Act 2, Sce 1:	Falsely accused and sentenced to death, he addresses a crowd in the street.

BUCKINGHAM:

All good people,
You that thus far have come to pity me,
Hear what I say, and then go home and lose° me.
I have this day received a traitor's judgment,
And by that name must die: yet, heaven bear witness,
And if I have a conscience, let it sink me,
Even as the axe falls, if I be not faithful!
The law I bear no malice for my death;
'T has done, upon the premises,° but justice:
But those that sought it I could wish more° Christians:
Be what they will, I heartily forgive 'em:
Yet let 'em look° they glory not in mischief,
Nor build their evils on the graves of great men;
For then my guiltless blood must cry against 'em.
For further life in this world I ne'er hope,
Nor will I sue,° although the king have mercies
More than I dare make faults. You few that loved me,
And dare be bold to weep for Buckingham,
His noble friends and fellows, whom to leave
Is only bitter to him, only dying,
Go with me, like good angels, to my end;
And, as the long divorce° of steel falls on me,
Make of your prayers one sweet sacrifice,°
And lift my soul to heaven. Lead on, o' God's name.

lose: forget. *sue*: appeal, petition. *premises:* evidence. *more:* truer.
look: beware. *divorce of steel*: beheading; i.e. the separation between
life and death. *sacrifice*: addition, a prayer for me.

HENRY VIII

by William Shakespeare

Character:	Duke of Buckingham, male. Honorable yet quick-tempered. He has a deep loathing of his enemies.
Playing age:	40s – 50s.
Act 2, Sce 1:	Addressing a crowd in a London street while being taken to his execution, Buckingham talks of betrayal; the similarity of his fate to that of his father; and cautions against speaking freely in the company of those that might betray you.

BUCKINGHAM:
When I came hither, I was lord high constable
And Duke of Buckingham; now, poor Edward Bohun:
Yet I am richer than my base accusers,
That never knew what truth meant: I now seal it;
And with that blood will make 'em one day groan for't.
My noble father, Henry of Buckingham,
Who first raised head° against usurping Richard,
Flying for succor to his servant Banister,
Being distressed, was by that wretch betrayed,
And without trial fell; God's peace be with him!
Henry the Seventh succeeding, truly pitying
My father's loss, like a most royal prince,
Restored me to my honours, and, out of ruins,
Made my name once more noble. Now his son,
Henry the Eighth, life, honour, name and all
That made me happy at one stroke has taken
Forever from the world. I had my trial,
And, must needs say, a noble one; which makes me,
A little happier than my wretched father:
Yet thus far we are one in fortunes: both
Fell by our servants, by those men we loved most;
A most unnatural and faithless service!
Heaven has an end° in all: yet, you that hear me,
This from a dying man receive as certain:
Where you are liberal of your loves and counsels

Be sure you be not loose; for those you make friends
And give your hearts to, when they once perceive
The least rub° in your fortunes, fall away
Like water from ye, never found again
But where they mean to sink ye. All good people,
Pray for me! I must now forsake ye: the last hour
Of my long weary life is come upon me. Farewell:
And when you would say something that is sad,
Speak how I fell. I have done; and God forgive me!

head: army. *end*: purpose. *rub*: obstacle.

THE DUCHESS OF MALFI
by John Webster

Character:	Bosola, male. A character full of complexities: a malcontent, a spy, a plain talker, and a convicted murderer who is remorseful about his part in the Duchess' death. Bosola is the henchman with a conscience but not before he has murdered everyone.
Playing age:	30s – 50s.
Act 4, Sce 2:	Pretending to be her coffin maker, Bosola enters the Duchess' cell where he slowly reveals his true purpose: to oversee her execution.

BOSOLA:

Thou? Art a box of worm-seed, at best but a salvatory° of green mummy.° What's this flesh? A little crudded milk, fantastical puff-paste. Our bodies are weaker than those paper prisons boys use to keep flies in, more contemptible since ours is to preserve earthworms. Didst thou ever see a lark in a cage? Such is the soul in the body: this world is like her little turf of grass, and the heaven o'er our heads like her looking-glass, only gives us a miserable knowledge of the small compass of our prison.

Thou art some great woman, sure, for riot begins to sit on thy forehead (clad in gray hairs) twenty years sooner than on a merry milk-maid's. Thou sleepest worse than if a mouse should be forced to take up her lodging in a cat's ear: a little infant that breeds its teeth, should it lie with thee, would cry out, as if thou wert the more unquiet bedfellow.

[Enter executioners.]

Here is a present from your princely brothers;
And may it arrive welcome, for it brings
Last benefit, last sorrow.

salvatory: tincture. *green mummy*: not quite ripe enough to be a corpse.

Martin Jago

THE DUCHESS OF MALFI
by John Webster

Character:	The Duchess, female. A strong, defiant, and passionate woman with power.
Playing age:	20s – 30s.
Act 4, Sce 2:	She faces her execution by strangling with great dignity and stoicism. Asked by Bosola if she fears death or the nature of it, she gives her answer.

DUCHESS:

What would it pleasure me to have my throat cut
With diamonds? Or to be smothered
With cassia? Or to be shot to death, with pearls?
I know death hath ten thousand several doors
For men to take their exits; and 'tis found
They go on such strange geometrical hinges,
You may open them both ways: any way, for Heaven sake,
So I were out of your whispering. Tell my brothers
That I perceive death, now I am well awake,
Best gift is they can give or I can take.
I would fain put off my last woman's fault,
I'd not be tedious to you.

Dispose my breath how please you; but my body
Bestow upon my women, will you?
Pull, and pull strongly, for your able strength
Must pull down heaven upon me:
Yet stay, heaven gates are not so highly arched
As princes' palaces: they that enter there
Must go upon their knees. [*She kneels.*] Come violent death,
Serve for mandragora° to make me sleep.
Go tell my brothers, when I am laid out,
They then may feed in quiet.

mandragora: mandrake root, a drug.

THE DUCHESS OF MALFI
by John Webster

Character: Bosola, male. A character full of complexities: a
                malcontent, a spy, a plain talker, and a convicted
                murderer who is remorseful about his part in the
                Duchess' death. Bosola is the henchman with a
                conscience but not before murdering everyone.

Playing age: 30s – 50s.

Act 4, Sce 2:   After her execution, the Duchess' brother betrays
                Bosola in whose service he committed the crime.
                He expresses true remorse only to discover she is
                still alive. She is briefly revived before dying.

BOSOLA:

Oh, she's gone again: there the cords° of life broke.
Oh sacred innocence, that sweetly sleeps
On turtles' feathers, whilst a guilty conscience
Is a black register wherein is writ
All our good deeds and bad, a perspective
That shows us hell; that we cannot be suffered
To do good when we have a mind to it!
This is manly sorrow;
These tears, I am very certain, never grew
In my mother's milk. My estate is sunk
Below the degree of fear: where were
These penitent fountains while she was living?
Oh, they were frozen up! Here is a sight
As direful to my soul as is the sword
Unto a wretch hath slain his father.
Come, I'll bear thee hence,
And execute thy last will; that's deliver
Thy body to the reverend dispose
Of some good women: that the cruel tyrant
Shall not deny me. Then I'll post to Milan,
Where somewhat I will speedily enact
Worth my dejection.°

cords: veins, arteries. ***dejection***: low status.

THE TWO NOBLE KINSMEN
by John Fletcher and William Shakespeare

Character:	The Jailer's Daughter, female. A tender young woman, deeply romantic and madly in love with Palamon for whom she is willing to give up her virginity.
Playing age:	Late teens.
Act 2, Sce 4:	The prison. She enters alone and talks of how her heart has been captured by the captive Palamon.

JAILER'S DAUGHTER:

Why should I love this gentleman? 'Tis odds
He will never affect° me. I am base,
My father the mean° keeper of his prison,
And he a prince. To marry him is hopeless,°
To be his whore is witless. Out upon't,
What pushes° are we wenches driven to
When fifteen once has found us? First, I saw him;
I, seeing, thought he was a goodly man;
He has as much to please a woman in him—
If he please to bestow it so—as ever
These eyes yet looked on. Next, I pitied him,
And so would any young wench, o'my conscience,
That ever dreamed or vowed her maidenhead°
To a young handsome man. Then, I loved him,
Extremely loved him, infinitely loved him—
And yet he had a cousin fair as he, too.
But in my heart was Palamon, and there,
Lord, what a coil° he keeps! To hear him
Sing in an evening, what a heaven it is!
And yet his songs are sad ones. Fairer spoken
Was never gentleman. When I come in
To bring him water in a morning, first
He bows his noble body, then salutes me, thus:
'Fair, gentle maid, good morrow. May thy goodness
Get thee a happy husband.' Once he kissed me—
I loved my lips the better ten days after.

Would he would do so every day! He grieves much,
And me as much to see his misery.
What should I do to make him know I love him?
For I would fain° enjoy° him. Say I ventured
To set him free? What says the law then? Thus much
For law or kindred! I will do it,
And this night; ere° tomorrow he shall love me.

affect: love. ***mean***: poor. ***hopeless***: beyond hope. ***pushes***: extremities
maidenhead: virginity. ***coil***: turmoil. ***fain***: happily. ***enjoy***: love, make
love to. ***ere***: before.

THE TWO NOBLE KINSMEN
by John Fletcher and William Shakespeare

Character:	The Jailer's Daughter, female. A tender young woman, deeply romantic and madly in love with Palamon for whom she is willing to give up her virginity.
Playing age:	Late teens.
Act 2, Sce 6:	The prison. The Jailer's Daughter has taken a great risk in releasing Palamon from prison. She hopes it will help win his heart.

JAILER'S DAUGHTER:
Let all the dukes and all the devils roar—
He is at liberty! I have ventured° for him,
And out I have brought him. To a little wood
A mile hence I have sent him, where a cedar
Higher than all the rest spreads like a plane,
Fast by a brook—and there he shall keep close°
Till I provide him files and food, for yet
His iron bracelets° are not off. O Love,
What a stout-hearted child thou art! My father
Durst better have endured cold iron than done it.
I love him beyond love and beyond reason
Or wit or safety. I have made him know it—
I care not, I am desperate. If the law
Find me and then condemn me for't, some wenches,
Some honest-hearted maids, will sing my dirge°
And tell to memory° my death was noble,
Dying almost a martyr. That way he takes,
I purpose,° is my way too. Sure, he cannot
Be so unmanly as to leave me here.
If he do, maids will not so easily
Trust men again. And yet, he has not thanked me
For what I have done—no, not so much as kissed me—
And that, methinks, is not so well. Nor scarcely
Could I persuade him to become a free man,
He made such scruples of the wrong he did

To me and to my father. Yet, I hope
When he considers more, this love of mine
Will take more root within him. Let him do
What he will with me—so he use me kindly.°
For use me, so he shall, or I'll proclaim him,
And to his face, no man. I'll presently
Provide him with necessaries and pack my clothes up,
And where there is a patch of ground I'll venture,
So he be with me. By him, like a shadow,
I'll ever dwell. Within this hour the hubbub
Will be all o'er the prison—I am then
Kissing the man they look for. Farewell, father,
Get many more such prisoners and such daughters,
And shortly you may keep° yourself. Now to him.

ventured: risked. *close:* secretly. *bracelets:* manacles. *dirge:* funeral
song. *memory:* history. *purpose:* plan. *kindly:* lovingly. *keep:* guard.

THE TWO NOBLE KINSMEN
by John Fletcher and William Shakespeare

Character:	The Jailer's Daughter, female. A tender young woman, deeply romantic and madly in love with Palamon for whom she is willing to give up her virginity.
Playing age:	Late teens.
Act 3, Sce 4:	The Jailer's Daughter continues to search for her love Palamon while wandering through the forest searching for food. She has lost her mind, singing a song as she goes.

JAILER'S DAUGHTER:
I am very cold, and all the stars are out too,
The little stars and all that, that look like aglets°—
The sun has seen my folly. Palamon!
Alas, no, he's in heaven. Where am I now?
Yonder's the sea and there's a ship—how't tumbles!
And there's a rock lies watching under water—
Now, now, it beats upon it—now, now, now,
There's a leak sprung, a sound° one—how they cry!
Set her before the wind—you'll lose all else.
Up with a course or two and tack about, boys.
Good night, good night, you're gone. I am very hungry.
Would I could find a fine frog—he would tell me
News from all parts o' th' world, then would I make
A carrack° of a cockle-shell, and sail
By east and north-east to the King of Pygmies,
For he tells fortunes rarely.° Now my father,
Twenty to one, is trussed up in a trice
Tomorrow morning. I'll say never a word.

   [She sings.]

For I'll cut my green coat, a foot above my knee,
And I'll clip my yellow locks, an inch below mine eye,
Hey nonny, nonny, nonny,

He s'buy me a white cut,° forth for to ride,
And I'll go seek him, through the world that is so wide,
Hey nonny, nonny, nonny
O for a prick now, like a nightingale,
To put my breast against. I shall sleep like a top else.

aglet: dress pin, brooch. ***sound:*** large. ***carrack:*** large ship. ***rarely:*** excellently. ***cut:*** workhorse.

THE DEVIL IS AN ASS

by Ben Jonson

Character:	Pug. A simple, inferior devil who persuades Satan to send him to earth.
Playing age:	Any age.
Act 5, Sce 2:	Pug, a devil, has been beaten, abused, and imprisoned. He'd prefer hell to another day in London with its degenerate (if not fashionable) inhabitants.

PUG:

O call me home again, dear chief, and put me
To yoking foxes, milking of he-goats,
Pounding of water in a mortar, laving
The sea dry with a nutshell, gathering all
The leaves are fallen this autumn, drawing farts
Out of dead bodies, making ropes of sand,
Catching the winds together in a net,
Mustering of ants, and numbering atoms; all
That hell and you thought exquisite torments, rather
Than stay me here a thought more: I would sooner
Keep fleas within a circle, and be accomptant°
A thousand year which of 'em and how far
Out-leaped the other, than endure a minute
Such as I have within. There is no hell
To a lady of fashion. All your tortures there
Are pastimes to it. 'Twould be a refreshing
For me to be i'the fire again, from hence.
To Newgate° brought? How is the name of the devil
Discredited in me! What a lost fiend
Shall I be on return! My chief will roar
In triumph now that I have been on earth
A day and done no noted thing, but brought
That body back here was hanged out this morning.

accomptant: keep account, record. *Newgate*: Newgate Prison.

THE OLD LAW
by Thomas Middleton and William Rowley

Character:	Creon, male. An honorable old man who has lived a good life.
Playing age:	Late 70s – 80.
Act 1, Sce 1:	A new euthanasia law decrees that every man who reaches the age of eighty years of age must be put to death and thrown into the sea from a clifftop. Creon is rapidly approaching his eightieth year and is outraged at the law. Here, he talks of his rich and full life and how having survived so much, it is wrong that a tyrannical law should end his life and change the course of destiny.

CREON:
Sorrow for what, Antigona, for my life?
My sorrow's° I have kept it so long well
With bringing it up unto so ill an end.
I might have gently lost it in my cradle,
Before my nerves and ligaments grew strong
To bind it faster to me. In my youth
I was a soldier, no coward in my age;
I never turned my back upon my foe.
I have felt nature's winter sicknesses,
Yet ever kept a lively sap in me
To greet the cheerful spring of health again.
Dangers on horseback, on foot, by water,
I have 'scaped to this day; and yet this day,
Without all help of casual° accidents,
Is only deadly to me 'cause it numbers
Fourscore years to me. Where's the fault now?
I cannot blame time, nature, nor my stars,
Nor aught but tyranny. Even kings themselves
Have sometimes tasted an even° fate with me.
He that has been a soldier all his days,
And stood in personal opposition
'Gainst darts and arrows, extremes of heat,

And pinching cold, has treacherously at home
In his secured quiet, by a villain's hand
Been basely lost in his star's ignorance;
And so must I die by a tyrant's sword.

sorrow's: sorrow is. ***casual***: random, unexpected. ***even***: exactly the
same.

THE OLD LAW
by Thomas Middleton and William Rowley

Character:	Hippolita, female. Honorable, virtuous, and a little naïve.
Playing age:	30s – 40s.
Act 5, Sce 1:	During the play's finale, a trial scene, Hippolita, the daughter-in-law of Creon, an old man shortly to be put to death as a result of Draconian euthanasia laws, addresses the judges in the case.

HIPPOLITA:

Alas, I know not how to style° you yet;
To call you judges doth not suit your years,
Nor heads and beards show more antiquity.
Yet sway yourselves with equity and truth
And I'll proclaim you reverend—and repeat,

"Once in my lifetime I have seen grave heads
Placed on young men's shoulders."

So prove not monstrous,
For yet, methinks, you bear the shapes of men,
Though nothing more than mercy beautifies
To make you appear angels. But if you crimson°
Your name and power with blood and cruelty,
Suppress fair virtue and enlarge of old vice,°
Both against heaven and nature draw your sword,
Make either will or humour° turn the soul
Of your created greatness—and in that
Oppose all goodness—I must tell you there
You're more than monstrous. In the very act,
You change yourself to devils.

style: judge, call. *crimson*: shame. *enlarge…vice*: increase your vices.
humour: temperament.

THE QUEEN OF CORINTH
by John Fletcher, Nathan Field, and Philip Massinger

Character:	Marshal, male. An officer of the law. Astute, observant, and conspiratorial.
Playing age:	30s – 50s.
Act 5, Sce 4:	Before the court proceedings are under way the Marshal reports to Euphanes on the behavior of the prisoners during their incarceration. In particular, he reports on how the prince's behavior contrasted to the others, clearly revealing his guilt.

MARSHAL:
Your brother,
With the other courtiers, willingly received
All courtesies I could offer; eat and drank,
And were exceeding merry, so dissembling°
Their guilt, or confident in their innocence,
That I much wondered at it. But the prince,
That, as born highest, should have graced his fall
With greatest courage, is so sunk with sorrow,
That to a common judgment he would seem
To suffer like a woman; but to me,
That from the experience I have had of many,
Look further in him, I do find the deep
Consideration of what's past more frights him
Than any other punishment.

I pressed to him,
And notwithstanding the queen's strict command
(Having your lordship's promise to secure me),
Offered to free him from his bonds, which he
Refused with such a sorrow, mixed with scorn,
That it amazed me; yet I urged his highness
To give one reason for't: He briefly answered,
That he had sat in judgment on himself,
And found that he deserved them;° that he was

A ravisher,° and so to suffer like one;
"Which is the reason of my tears," he addeth,
"For were't not I again should break the laws
By scorning all their rigour can inflict,
I should die smiling."°

dissembling: concealing, disguising. *them*: the judgements, sentence.
ravisher: rapist. *for were't…smiling*: I would die happy by accepting
rather than scorning the harsh reality of the law, i.e. my punishment
by death.

Martin Jago

THE QUEEN OF CORINTH
by John Fletcher, Nathan Field, and Philip Massinger

Character:	Beliza, female. A lady of the court. Strong and independent.
Playing age:	20s – 30s.
Act 5, Sce 4:	In court Beliza argues for her rapist's death. The law states if a victim marries him, he may be pardoned. Another victim, Merione, has agreed to this. Beliza strongly rebukes her and rails against the law.

BELIZA:
Is that justice?
Shall one that is to suffer for a rape
Be by a rape defended? Look upon
The public enemy of chastity,
This lustful satyr, whose enraged desires
The ruin of one wretched virgin's honour
Would not suffice, and shall the wreck of two
Be his protection? Maybe I was ravished°
For his lust only, thou for his defence;
Oh, fine evasion!° Shall with such a slight°
Your justice be deluded?° Your laws cheated?
And be that for one fact deserved to die,
For sinning often, find impunity?°
But that I know thee, I would swear thou wert
A false impostor, and suborned° to this:
And it may be thou art, Merione;
For hadst thou suffered truly what I have done,
Thou wouldst like me complain, and call for vengeance,
And, our wrongs being equal, I alone
Should not desire revenge, but be it so
If thou prevail, even he will punish it,°
And foolish mercy showed to him undo thee.
Consider, fool, before it be too late,
What joys thou canst expect from such a husband,

To whom thy first, and what's more, forced embraces,
Which men say heighten pleasure, were distasteful.

ravished: raped. *fine evasion*: expression of incredulity that one should evade justice in such a way. *slight*: trick. *deluded*: deceived. *impunity*: immunity. *suborned*: bribed. *even...punish it*: being even, that is equal in law, acquitted, he will punish you.

THE QUEEN OF CORINTH
by John Fletcher, Nathan Field, and Philip Massinger

Character:	Queen, female. A wise and virtuous widow. Disgusted by the lechery of her son.
Playing age:	40s – 50s.
Act 5, Sce 4:	The Queen sentences her own son Theanor to death for double rape. In doing so, she satisfies one woman, Beliza, and devastates another, Merione.

QUEEN:

Merione, I could wish I were no queen,
To give you satisfaction; no mother,
Beliza, to content you; and would part
Even with my being, both might have their wishes;
But since that is impossible, in few words
I will deliver what I am resolved on.
The end for which all profitable° laws
Were made looks two ways only, the reward
Of innocent good men, and the punishment
Of bad delinquents: Ours, concerning rapes,
Provided that same latter clause of marriage
For him that had fall'n once, not then foreseeing
Mankind could prove so monstrous to tread twice
A path so horrid. The great lawgiver
Draco, that for his strange severity
Was said to write his stern decrees in blood,
Made none for parricides,° presuming that
No man could be so wicked: Such might be
Lycurgus'° answer, did he live, for this.
But since I find that in my son which was not
Doubted in any else, I will add to it:
He cannot marry both, but for both dying,
Both have their full revenge. You see, Beliza,
You have your wish. With you, Merione,
I'll spend a tear or two. So, Heaven forgive thee.

profitable: good. **parricides**: murder of a parent. **Lycurgus**: Ancient Greek strict lawmaker.

THE FATAL DOWRY

by Philip Massinger and Nathan Field

Character:	Romont, male. A fiery character. Outspoken, quick-tempered, and fiercely loyal.
Playing age:	30s.
Act 1, Sce 2:	Romont rails against the court in defense of his friend Charalois, berating and cursing the judges for not allowing the body of his friend's father to be released from prison and buried.

ROMONT:
If that curses,
Urged justly,° and breathed forth so, ever fell
On those that did deserve them, let not mine
Be spent in vain now, that thou, from this instant,
Mayest in thy fear that they will fall upon thee,
Be sensible of the plagues they shall bring with them.
And for denying of a little earth
To cover what remains of our great soldier
May all your wives prove whores, your factors° thieves,
And while you live, your riotous heirs undo you,
And thou, the patron of their cruelty.
Of all thy lordships live not to be owner
Of so much dung as will conceal a dog,
Or what is worse, thyself in. And thy years,
To th' end thou mayest be wretched, I wish many,
And as thou hast denied the dead a grave,
May misery in thy life make thee desire one,
Which men and all the elements keep from thee:

[Aside to Charalois.]

I have begun well, imitate, exceed.°

urged justly: justifiably spoken. **factors**: financial/business partners.
imitate, exceed: he is suggesting that Charalois speak next and build on the fine defense he has just made.

THE FATAL DOWRY
by Philip Massinger and Nathan Field

Character:	Charalois, male. A noble gentleman full of honor, valor, and eloquence.
Playing age:	Late 20s – 30.
Act 1, Sce 2:	Charalois' father, went into debt and died in jail. His creditors won't release his body. Charalois addresses the court and the creditors. He offers to pay the debt by taking his father's place in prison, allowing the body to be released and buried.

CHARALOIS:

O since you are as merciless in your natures,
As base and mercenary in your means
By which you get your wealth, I will not urge
The court to take away one scruple from
The right of their laws or wish one good thought
In you to mend your disposition with.
I know there is no music to your ears
So pleasing as the groans of men in prison,
And that the tears of widows, and the cries
Of famished orphans, are the feasts that take° you.
That to be in your danger, with more care
Should be avoided than infectious air,
The loathed embraces of diseased women,
A flatterer's poison° or the loss of honour.
Yet, rather than my father's reverend dust
Shall want° a place in that fair monument
In which our noble ancestors lie intombed,
Before the court I offer up myself
A prisoner for it. Load me with those irons°
That have worn out his life; in my best strength
I'll run to the encounter of cold, hunger,
And choose my dwelling where no sun dares enter,
So may he be released.

take: captivate. *poison*: i.e. believe what flatterers say. *want*: not have.
irons: shackles.

CAROLINE AGE (1625 – 1649)

THE ROMAN ACTOR
by John Massinger

Character:	Paris, male. An accomplished actor. and dignified.
Playing age:	20s – 40s.
Act 1, Sce 3:	Accused of treason for being an actor, and thereby '*traduce persons of rank*' and '*make even the senators ridiculous to the plebeians,*' Paris. Eloquently defends himself in court.

PARIS:
When do we bring a vice upon the stage
That does go off unpunished? Do we teach,
By the success of wicked undertakings,
Others to tread in their forbidden steps?
Even those spectators that were so inclined
Go home changed men. And for traducing° such
That are above us, publishing to the world
Their secret crimes we are as innocent
As such as are born dumb. When we present
An heir that does conspire against the life
Of his dear parent, numbering every hour
He lives as tedious to him, if there be
Among the auditors° one whose conscience tells him
He is of the same mould, we cannot help it.
Or bringing on the stage a loose adulteress
That does maintain the riotous expense
Of him that feeds her greedy lust, yet suffers
The lawful pledges of a former bed
To starve the while for hunger—if a matron,
However great in fortune, birth or titles,
Guilty of such a foul unnatural sin,
Cry out ''tis writ by me,' we cannot help it.
Or when we show a judge that is corrupt,
And will give up his sentence as he favours
The person, not the cause, saving the guilty,

If of his faction, and as oft condemning
The innocent out of particular spleen,°
If any in this reverend assembly,
Nay, e'en yourself my Lord, that are the image
Of absent Caesar feel something in your bosom
That puts you in remembrance of things past,
Or things intended, 'tis not in us to help it.
I have said, my Lord, and now, as you find cause,
Or censure us, or free us with applause.

traducing: slandering. *auditors*: audience. *spleen*: anger.

INDEX

ABOUT THE AUTHOR

Martin Jago is an interdisciplinary theatre director from Great Britain with a passion for classical plays, contemporary plays, and new writing.

The author of several plays and two previous books on Shakespeare published by *Smith & Kraus,* he is delighted to continue his partnership with one of the world's foremost publishers of theatre trade books.

The Founding Artistic Director of RAZE THE SPACE, a Los Angeles based theatre company with a global perspective, he maintains a vibrant working practice, enriched by the spirit of international collaboration that defines his work.

He was educated at the University of Oxford and The Royal Welsh College of Music and Drama.